THE MIRACLE OF
YOU

Also by Elaine L Wilson

Opening Doors

Until God So Wills

Let There Be Light

Messengers of Miracles

Coming Home

Transcending Time

The Passion of the Soul

Look to the Shore

Leaving Legacies

Present at the Table

Another World

A Second Chance

Iconically Speaking

Shining Lights

Amidst the Stars

In Praise

Other Shores

Your Favorite Guest

THE MIRACLE OF YOU

YOU ARE SO MUCH MORE THEN YOU EVER THOUGHT YOU WERE!

ELAINE L WILSON

Artwork and cover design: originals by Elaine L Wilson

Balboa Press books may be ordered through booksellers or by contacting:

Balboa Press
A Division of Hay House
1663 Liberty Drive
Bloomington, IN 47403
www.balboapress.com
1 (877) 407-4847

Printed in the United States of America.

ISBN: 978-1-4525-8300-6 (sc)
ISBN: 978-1-4525-8302-0 (hc)
ISBN: 978-1-4525-8301-3 (e)

Library of Congress Control Number: 2013917399

Balboa Press rev. date: 10/02/2013

To

My son,
STEVAN D WILSON, PHD

and

My friend,
JAMES P O'LEARY

Note to Readers

As you turn this book's pages, experiences and examples from your life could come to you. Miracles, inspirations, memories, and thoughts that are meant only for you pass through your mind all the time. Singular ideas visit you every day. Blank pages at the end of the book are waiting in the event you care to make notes.

"If we could see the miracle of a single flower clearly,
our whole life would change."
—Buddha

"The true miracle is not walking on water or walking
in air, but simply walking on this earth."
—Thich Nhat Hanh

"The only way to live is to accept each minute as an
unrepeatable miracle, which is exactly what it is:
a miracle and unrepeatable."
—Margaret Storm Jameson

"Miracles are a retelling in small letters of the very same story,
which is written across the whole world
in letters too large for some of us to see."
—C. S. Lewis

"Miracles: You do not have to look for them.
They are there, 24-7, beaming like radio waves all around you."
—Hugh Elliott

"To me every hour of the light and dark is a miracle.
Every cubic inch of space is a miracle."
—Walt Whitman

The Miracle of You

You are a miracle.
A priceless,
irreplaceable treasure.
You are here
by divine grace.
Equipped with
unique talents and intentions.
Care for yourself
with gentleness and
generosity.
Bathe your blessed soul
in the wonderment
that is you.
Rejoice!

No one can do what you can do.
No one can be as you are.
You are a gift to the world.
You ARE a miracle.

Contents

Preface

Born beyond the stars themselves,
your soul is destined for immortality.
You are in every sense nature's greatest joy.
And, you are God's greatest miracle.
Elaine Wilson shows you
how you came to be what you are
and
offers you infinite possibilities
for what you can become
in this amazing book called
The Miracle of You.

INTRODUCTION

We learn from our own experiences and from those who have gone before us. Therefore, in *The Miracle of You* I chose examples of well-known and not so well known people to frame points. They serve as flagships to illustrate what we choose to do with our miraculous lives can, more often than not, be achieved. Some of the individual's names and experiences "came to me" as I wrote. Others have always intrigued me. Still others have played significant roles in my personal life over the years.

On my part, no effort was made to balance the representative numbers of men to women. I elected to consider how lives were lived and what specific messages they delivered... not faiths, sexes, skin colors, nationalities, or ages. This book would be deemed "politically incorrect" on those accounts. However, I make no apologies. It is my persuasion that we are one with the Universe. God sees us as one. We *are* one with him. Consequently, individual's contributions mattered the most to me. My interests are those that bind us together as one human race, not those that separate us in senseless ways and on so many (unnecessary) levels.

The early chapters guide you through fascinating facts and details about the miracle that you are. They usher in miraculous experiences in the lives of others. Then the book moves on to an exploration of why knowing and living with joy is so absolutely paramount to your phenomenal Earth time tenure.

Maintaining a personal belief system is vital to your remarkable lifetime as well. An overview on "believing" is examined. Chapter 15 presents the concept of Pathways where ideas for developing a workable, personal, belief system are extended for your consideration. Suggestions and cautions are put forth to lend support to your odyssey.

Your time on Earth, your safari on this planet, provides awe-inspiring opportunities for you to explore Pathways designed specifically for you. Many were predestined by you for you to enrich your Earth time experiences. That planning happened long before you intentionally arrived here. Now those opportunities can and will lead you triumphantly back home. Hopefully you will travel through life blessed with multitudes of rewarding, fruitful, and joyous moments.

As a preliminary suggestion, while you read this book "listen" for the messages that are *not* on the printed pages. Listen for the messages that come into your amazing mind. Often information, which is truly *for* you, is beyond what is physically offered.

You are so much more than you ever thought you were. Enjoy and find joy in *The Miracle of You*.

Elaine L Wilson

1

You are a Miracle

You have many dimensions, all of them unique.

OVER 13 BILLION YEARS AGO our Universe began, born from what experts now believe was a tiny speck. Over time gravity appeared. Then Earth and the other planets, stars, and galaxies in our solar system were formed. Some stars stayed small. Others developed into gigantic masses. Curiously, the biggest stars in the Universe experience the shortest life spans. Fortunately our sun, which is a star, is not such a big one. Scientists project it should be okay for about 10 million more years, so we can relax for the time being.

Supernovas, which are the biggest stars, explode violently, burn quickly, and scatter themselves far and wide. Their explosions create cosmic particles called stardust. Stardust is loaded with almost all the elements that we know on Earth. They are the elements from which we are made. Our bodies use elements like copper, sulphur, magnesium, potassium, lithium, and iron. It is noteworthy that our bodies absolutely demand those elements to function. If a body lacks potassium it experiences dizziness, can collapse, and at the worst loses consciousness. If a body is low in magnesium the memory will be compromised. Read the label on a bottle of a vitamin pills. All the ingredients listed originated in outer space and are positively critical to maintaining a healthy physical life on Earth. Our bodies function on cosmic particles. They require the stardust that emanates from outer space.

Always fascinated with the Universe, the American architect R. Buckminster Fuller (1895-1983) gets credit for coining the name *"Spaceship Earth."* He often remarked he felt like he was,

... a passenger on Spaceship Earth.

Spaceship Earth travels at 60,000 miles an hour around the mother ship Sun, which is 92 million miles away. Not only does Earth travel forward, it spins on its axis at 1000 miles per hour. As Fuller observed,

That is a whole lot of spin and zip.

In 1968, Fuller wrote a book called *Operating Manual for Spaceship Earth.* In it he proposed the following observations,

In reality, the Sun, the Earth, and the Moon
are nothing else than a most fantastically well-designed
and space-programmed team of vehicles.
All of us are, always have been,
and so long as we exist, always will be
–nothing else but astronauts.

What an engaging concept to consider. The Universe and all its moving parts are a *"space-programmed team of vehicles."* No wonder Fuller habitually referred to our planet as Spaceship Earth.

Technically all the elements needed by our bodies originated in outer space; therefore we all came from outer space. We are *"nothing else but astronauts."* Astronauts composed of cosmic dust, which are products of the Universe. We truly are physically fashioned stardust forms.

Another curious fact is that in our Universe all the people, planets, and stars comprise only 4% of the matter. Only 4%, as can best be determined. Baffling as that is to scientists, the other 96% cannot be substantially documented. For that reason the rest of the vastness around us is unknown and thus unquantifiable at this time. What *is* out there and why?

As for our *exact* ages, and stretching the facts just a little bit, we are truly billions of years old. We are miraculously all part of one greater whole, the whole we call the Universe. Our common origin is known of as the Source, the Creator, God. We not only came from, but destiny calls us to return to, that greater whole. We return both physically and spiritually. As the energy of the Universe is self-sustaining, so our energy is indestructible. Likewise are the elements of our bodies. It is a verity that we will live forever. What miracles we are!

The mathematical genius Albert Einstein (!879-1955) once contemplatively made this popular observation about miracles,

There are only two ways to live your life.
One is as though nothing is a miracle.
The other is as though everything is a miracle.

Truly, "*...everything is a miracle*" and that includes you. The creation of your life brought millions of cosmic particles into alignment. Your existence prevails because of the Universe. The Universe sustains you. Although on loan from the Universe, stardust dedicatedly and generously supports the miraculous creature you are.

Equally important to keep in mind is that you are original. You are absolutely one-of-one. In fact, nothing in all of creation is a duplicate. Nothing. No mountain, or tree, or rabbit, no seashell, or rose is like anything else in its category. There will never be any nature-made two-of-a-kinds... ever. You are one hundred percent exclusive and so is everything else.

No one has, has ever had, or ever will have your fingerprints, your footprints, your eye scans, or your genetic makeup. What attentive care and love went into the creation of you. How wonderful to consider you are that amazingly miraculous. No one can ever be exactly like you. That is how special you are.

As part of his work and research on human uniqueness Dr. Roger John Williams (1893-1988) a biochemist, nutritionist, and research professor at the University of Texas in Austin, named folic acid and discovered the growth-promoting vitamin pantothenic acid. Williams also studied variations within the human species. However, his preference was to look inside the human body for deviations from the normal.

Over time Williams compiled 26 books. In 1967, he wrote a book about the physical uniqueness of every person. The book is called *You are Extraordinary.* Williams' research and work underpins a wedge of the theme of *The Miracle of You.* Here are several selected statements.

This book brings a simple personal
message to you, the reader.
If you peruse its pages,
you will realize that you are, indeed,
a remarkable and extraordinary person….
the only kind of people that exist or
have ever existed on this earth
are the individual kind….
those who are not approximately like anyone else….

Part of the fun of life is having
a real appreciation for other people
who are as distinctive in makeup as
we individually are.

Accepting the wide deviations apparent on the exterior of human bodies, Williams' research focused on the pronounced differences within our bodies. That is something we customarily give little thought to considering. Examples of Williams' findings include:

» The location of the stomach shifts up or down by 5 inches in the abdomen. It can be found nearer to, or lower than, the rib cage.

» The primary shapes of stomachs widely differ.

» The number of parathyroid glands varies from 2-12. Four is the normal number.

» The site where the spinal cord stops at the lower end in the vertebral column varies by 3 inches from one person to another.

» The width, branching, and curving degrees of the arteries vary with every person.

Textbooks only provide medical doctors and researchers with suggestions as to where to find body organs. The individual's body governs the exact shape and location of its specific organs. As Williams crisply observed,

Everyone is a deviate.

So, it is official, you are a miraculous *"deviate."* You are unique from the inside out and beyond. Even your handwriting differs from that of others. You can use the same writing tool, the same writing surface, and write the exact same sentence as everyone else. Each person's writing sample will be as different as they are.

Furthermore, biological parents have no control over their children's fingerprints, footprints, eye scans, or genetic makeup.

Add to that list the child's unique handwriting style, the length of their spinal cord, the number of parathyroid glands in their body, and a host of other deviations. If the opposite was the case, should a family suffer the tragic loss of a child, the parents could create an exact duplicate.

Speaking of creating duplicates. The famous, two-time, World Heavyweight Boxing Champion, George Foreman (1949-), named all five of his sons George, for whatever reason made sense to him. Therefore, the Foreman family includes: George Jr., George III, George IV, George V, and George VI. Plus, one of his daughters is named Georgette and another is named Leola George Foreman. Nonetheless, no two George Foreman's are alike, except for the name George. George's children are all one-of-a-kinds. Just like you, just like your children, and your family.

My Father's family included twelve children. Although they all bore strong resemblances to their Swedish-born, American parents no two were, or looked, exactly alike. Herbert, Harry, and John did not look like or have exactly the same interests as Clarence, Wilbur, or Gerald. Mildred, Ellen, and Nina did not look or act like Gladys or Arlyne. While my Father did not look or act exactly like any of his siblings. Each of the twelve had their own amassed stardust elements, organic structure, and uniqueness.

Even identical twins mirror image each other. They are not exactly alike. No brothers and sisters, no sets of twins, and no two of us are alike. Not even if all of us have the same name.

Pablo Casals (1876-1973), the first-rate conductor and pre-eminent cellist of the first half of the 20th Century, firmly believed in mankind's uniqueness. On the topic he once observed,

The child must know that he is a miracle,
that since the beginning of the world
there hasn't been,
and until the end of the world there will not be,
another child like him.

However Casals believed that through the common voice of music people of all languages, political persuasions, and nationalities could be reached and united. Working in such a responsive and delicately interpretive artistic field, Casals placed high value on the exceptionalness of each individual.

We have all been children. And, as Casals pointed out, *"Until the end of the world"* there will never be *"another child like (you)."* We are living miracles. Our bodies, our minds, our spiritual forces, and our astronaut stardust makeups all qualify for that same exclusiveness. No one else is, or ever will be you, or you, or you. How totally awe-inspiring that is.

Our extraordinary bodies are entire *"systems of miracles"* as author and inspirational lecturer, Dr. Wayne W Dyer (1940-), called them. To further support your distinctive miracle status, here is a simplistic example of one aspect of what your *"system(s) of miracles"* can do.

If I get a little cut on my hand, my body immediately goes about the business of healing the wound. I do not have to "tell it" to do anything. My beating heart sends blood rushing through my veins and arteries bringing the necessary elements to assist in healing the small cut. All the while, aside from applying a Band-Aid to the site, I give no thought to the magical healing process going on within me, in my *"system(s) of miracles."* I calmly drink a cup of coffee, chat on the phone, or sit back enjoying a good book. I am confident my body will heal itself. And, miraculously it does.

You ingest food and your entire digestive system pounces into action. Every day your immune system goes out on patrol checking to keep all of you running smoothly, thus avoiding physical complications that could lead to illnesses, overt stresses, or diseases. While at the same time your body grows hair and fingernails and your lungs take in and release air to cleanse and energize your body. Now that is impressive.

The human body contains over 50 trillion cells. Over a period of seven years every cell in the body is replaced. Approximately 98% of the atoms in your body are replaced every 3-6 months. Your subconscious manages all those functions. You do not "will," cannot control, and never even consider attempts to manage any aspect of those critical activities. You are an everlasting miracle of the highest order.

Just as the Source imagined the Universe into being from the vastness of void, he imagined each of us. He imagined us long before our physical births on Earth. Within our minds we encompass the vastness of space, while our souls enjoy the limitlessness of forever. As you will be reminded, we do not destruct. Our bodies are temporal. *We* are not.

And, to be scientifically correct, we are actually not physical bodies. The pulsing energies of the Universe's vibrations and gravitational pull are so strong they hold our bodies into forms. Those forms house our minds and the everlasting souls that we are. We are souls, miraculous souls, souls who have all emanated from the Universe, the Source. We are all one.

On the topic of oneness, consider the following,

You are one.
Mankind is one.
The Earth is one.

The Universe is one.
All are one.

As your body has many facets,
so the world and beyond.
But it is all one.
When you move you
take all of you with you.
As does the earth.
As does the Universe.
You are one.
Many parts of one.
One that is greater than all its parts.
The Earth is greater than all its parts.
The Universe is greater than all its parts.
The Universe is one with God.
God, the Source, the Universe are all one.

Oneness and miracles are what the Universe is all about and what you are all about. You are a single, exclusive miracle of the highest order. In the next chapter a critical component of your being will be explored. That component is your fascinating mind.

2

WHERE IS YOUR MIND?

When you "get right down to it" everything you perceive and achieve hinges on how you think.

SINCE THE DAWN OF RECORDED history, societies have been intrigued with the human mind. Within one generation families will have members who are born gifted, obsessed, compromised, and/or a myriad of other categories. Unlike the physical body, the mind is not created from inherited genes.

Where *is* your mind? You know where your brain is, but where is your mind? Where is the biological structure that holds the thoughts that make you who you are? Or, is the mind a biological structure? How large an area does it comprise inside your head or your body? Where is its verifiable power center? Was it born with you? Or, has it been with you always? How do you get a grip on the shape and scope of the mind? Or… is that possible?

In biblical times multitudes flocked to hear Jesus of Nazareth speak. Some came for the messages; others were carried to see him because of their sufferings. They sought his presence and powers in the hope he could heal them. Along with curing blindness, deafness, osteoporosis, epilepsy, paralysis, and physical deformities, Jesus drove demons out of distressed minds. The Apostle John (6-100 AD) recorded one of many such incidents in *The New Testament*. In the book of John 20:9, he wrote,

Now when Jesus was risen early
the first day of the week,
he appeared first to Mary Magdalene,
out of whom he had cast seven devils.

Early in Jesus' ministry a woman named Mary Magdalene

walked from her city of Magdala along the Mediterranean Sea. She came to the area around the Sea of Galilee in search of him. Supposedly her mental demons came and went at will from her mind. Overpowering her physically and emotionally when they surfaced, they kept her in a constant state of insecurity and fear. She believed Jesus could drive out her demons. And, as John recorded, Jesus did.

Mental health issues have concerned people for centuries. Fortunately the variety of treatments offered in the 21st Century exceeds those available in the time of Jesus. Nowadays most troubled or anxious individuals who are looking for support will schedule appointments with psychiatrists, psychotherapists, or psychologists to talk about what is going on in their minds. Those patients share their fears, phobias, and disconnectednesses with the specialists or family doctors. However, they do not consider their appointments to be avenues toward having *"devils"* cast out. Sometimes, after a battery of evaluations, the professionals direct pharmacists to fill prescriptions designed to medicate mind-related issues. Additionally, therapeutic support group sessions exist to assist people in dealing with ages-old mental *"devils."* Devils that reside in the mind, where ever the mind actually is.

Schools and universities regularly test perspective students prior to admitting them. They want to be sure the students are placed at levels of instruction that will both challenge and stimulate their thinking, stretch their minds. Designed to evaluate mental aptitudes in a variety of arenas, the resulting data customarily provides fairly accurate numbers. Curiously, the tests are designed to produce results about what resides in a shapeless, space-less region no one has ever seen.

The word "mind" cannot be substituted or confused with the word "brain." Even dictionaries shy away from calling the actual brain "the mind." The brain's functions are critical to the orchestration of the entire physical body. X-rays distinctly reveal its soft, nervous tissue structure. However, x-rays never display an organic shape anywhere in the human body that is called the mind. And no donor-recipient list exists for mind transplants. The mind is not the brain. It is of the brain, but not the brain. Obviously invisible, and thus untouchable, still the mind controls, defines, and directs our lives on Earth on a multitude of essential levels.

The earlier question returns for consideration. Where is your mind?

While not listed in any of the systems categories that constitute the organs of the human body, the mind is unquestionably real. But, like the Universe from whence we have all come, its shape is as shapeless as that void. Yet, our mind underpins us from birth to death.

» It communicates in words we understand and in our voice.
» It persists with us when we are awake or asleep.
» It transfers and receives telepathic and intuitive messages.
» It generates emotional reactions.
» It warns of dangers and recognizes love and loved ones.
» It learns, understands, suspects, cares, prompts, and guides.
» It listens and evaluates the voices beyond us and it hears the voice within us.

As the active nurturer of all our thoughts, reactions, and creations the shapeless, space-less mind's power serves us well.

The phrases *"body and soul"* and *"mind and body"* reinforce an important point. Society views the body separate from the mind and the soul. The body *is* where ever you are physically. However, the mind is able to wander. You can be sitting in a car at a traffic light, while your mind reviews the dinner menu for the week, the last time you saw so-and-so, or the best day to get your haircut. Also in concert with your eyes, your mind watches for the light to change. Your mind imagines, inspires, creates, dreams, and faces reality. It functions in a wide spectrum of different arenas.

If you lose a limb or an organ such as your appendix, a kidney, or an eye, your body moves to make accommodations. If you get accidentally burned, scratched, or maimed, your body rushes into healing mode. Your body makes adjustments for what was lost or harmed. However, none of those incidents obligate your mind to be any less, any more, or any different than it was prior to the accident or surgery. Your independent mind continues to function. It avails itself of the body for "residential purposes," but it does not need a whole and perfect body to function. Yet, your body does not function at efficient levels without your mind. How curious and amazingly extraordinary you are.

The current-day television personality and British author of comedies and novels, Warren Ellis, (1968-) commented on this topic. In reflecting on questions about the brain, the mind, and thoughts Ellis posed his own question,

If you believe that your thoughts
originate inside your brain,
do you also believe
that television shows are made
inside your television set?

Ellis' question presents a humorous, but fascinating analogy. On a deeper and more serious level, inquisitive, theoretically inclined, philosophical men, from Aristotle to Plato to Immanuel

Kant to William James to Sigmund Freud and multitudes in between and after, have pondered the workings of the mind to no certain end. Mounds of research continue to be filed. Great thinkers have defined areas that involve the mind, such as personality, perception, and consciousness. Yet they have uncovered no concrete undisputable data as to the simplest question of all… where is the mind?

1. Your mind is a miracle like none other.
2. No one knows for certain how it works.
3. No one has ever seen a mind.

That having been established, the mind still enjoins a closer study. It impacts heavily on the miracle that is you. Where is the mind? Until further notice, the miraculous mind just "is."

The next chapter addresses a dimension of your mind referred to as "inspiration." All minds are gifted with moments of inspiration. Some of those moments bring about small but delightful surprises. Others have lead to remarkable inventions. While others have filled unsatisfied needs or under the umbrella heading of "progress" have advanced whole societies.

As you read the chapter appreciate how categorically essential inspiration is to living well. Be encouraged to freely act in those times when *you* receive messages from the other side, moments of inspiration. Realize absolutely nothing is impossible.

3

Minds that Made a Difference

The impact of your wave will ripple far into time.

WHENEVER THE WORD "MIND" IS mentioned, the name Albert Einstein immediately comes to the fore. Even as a child, the mysterious powers of the Universe tweaked his interest. As an adult, he spent the major part of his life "living and breathing" quantum physics and its theories.

In 1905, at the age of 26, the German-born American published a paper that contained his famous equation "$e=mc^2$." The equation's formula for energy-mass equivalence became the most famous equation in the world. With it, Dr. Einstein unlocked many of the secrets of the Universe.

Eleven years later, in 1916, he presented a work known as the Theory of Relativity. In 1917, Einstein applied his relativity theory to model a large-scale structure of our Universe. Acclaimed for the incredible acuity of his mind, Einstein's theory immediately replaced the 200-year old mechanical theory of Isaac Newton (1642-1727). Newton attested that gravity, inertia, and action-reaction laid the foundations for order in the Universe. With Einstein's advanced conclusions, theoretical physicists and scientists could more accurately predict the phenomena of astrophysics, such as neutron stars, black holes, and the waves of gravity.

Although revolutionary to the world of physics, Einstein believed his discoveries came from the simple act of refining his thinking, of using his mind to the utmost. On that topic, he once shared,

I have no special talents.
I am only passionately curious.

"Passionately curious" does not begin to explain the atypical functioning of Einstein's mind.

Einstein died at age 76, on April 18, 1955 in Princeton, New Jersey. The attending pathologist had always been impressed and intrigued with his patient's genius. Without prior legal permission from Einstein's family, he removed his brain for laboratory study. Naively the doctor hoped that over time scientists and medical researchers could learn what particular organic structures resided within Einstein's brain to gift him with such an extraordinary mathematical genius. Due to the doctor's action, at his death Einstein (Who was cremated.) left his brain. But Albert Einstein's mind left with him.

All the world's inventions and inspirations first originated in individual's minds. *Single* minds moved by the imagination of the spirit. Remarkably, as the needs of mankind have arisen, inspirational ideas came and continue to come.

Single creative notions have visited the minds of specifically targeted individuals throughout history. Individuals who, well in advance of their inspired thoughts and without foreknowledge that inspirations would come to them, found themselves miraculously equipped with the skills and the resolve to address the pending needs of their society. They acted on their ideas and thus met, and continue to meet, the necessities and desires of mankind.

In 1450, the German Johannes Gutenberg (1395-1468) was a goldsmith, blacksmith, printer, and publisher by trade. Around 1439, he figured out how to build a movable type printing press. Consider life before that invention. Every bit of information was either delivered via lip service, or by an official town crier, or in manuscript form after hours and hours of hand copying. His invention led to the spread of mass communication and played a significant role in ushering in the Renaissance and the effortlessness of modern learning.

In 1846, Elias Howe (1819-1867) patented the first, American, mechanical sewing machine. At 250 stitches a minute it could outdistance five, top, hand sewers in the same length of time. What a boon to the textile and clothing industries that machine and its successors became.

In 1935, while working for DuPont in Wilmington, Delaware, the chemist and inventor Wallace Hume Carothers (1896-1937) discovered how to turn fossil fuels into nylon. Nylon was the first entirely synthetic fiber made by man. His discovery arrived just in time. In the pre-World War II era, the United States' relations with Japan were collapsing. Nylon became a replacement for the Oriental silk we imported. Carothers is known as the Father of the Science of Manmade Polymers. Due to his invention, the world has never been the same since.

Many of the men and women who gifted mankind with the fruits of their imaginations felt humbled by their inventions. They resolutely affirmed their minds' geniuses lay beyond them. They believed the seeds of their efforts originated in that spaceless, shapeless, universal void they chose to call the Source, the Universe, God.

Another such genius was the American inventor, Thomas Alva Edison (1847-1931). Edison is recognized worldwide for his years of work and multitude of inventions in the field of electricity. His brilliance included a forerunner of today's music systems, the phonograph player. We also have him to thank for the first motion picture camera and, of course, the electric light bulb. During his lifetime he amassed 1093 patents. Until the 1920's when his health began to fail, he filed patent right applications for new inventions every two weeks. Edison's mind must have never stopped spinning. However appreciative we are for his creativity, Edison was fully aware of the Source of his inventions. He regularly and self-effacingly asserted,

I am a channel,
not the originator.

The 20th Century gave birth to countless inventions and discoveries through the minds of men and women on our planet. In December of 1901, an Italian progenitor named Guglielmo Marconi (1874-1937) sent the first long distance radio transmission across the Atlantic Ocean from Cornwall, England to St. John's, Newfoundland. In light of his inspired genius, the Nobel Prize winner and pioneer in long distance telegraph and radio transmission systems, was not without humility. In sharing his thoughts on the Universe, he once astutely remarked,

If we consider what science already
has enabled men to know
—the immensity of space,
the fantastic philosophy of the stars,
the infinite smallness of the composition of atoms,
the macrocosm whereby we succeed
only in creating outlines
and translating a measure into numbers
without our minds being able to form
any concrete idea of it—
we remain astounded by the enormous
machinery of the universe.

Marconi's perspectives on *"the enormous machinery of the Universe," "without our minds being able to form any concrete idea(s)*

of it" is philosophically written. Marconi's observations on his theories of life included,

> *The mystery of life is certainly the most*
> *persistent problem ever placed*
> *before the thought of man… .*
> *The inability of science to solve it is absolute.*
> *This would be truly frightening*
> *were it not for faith.*

"The inability of science" to totally comprehend *"the mystery of life"* is as true today as it was when Marconi penned it. Try as they will those who believe the minds of men can come to understand everything there is to know about life would do well to read the message found in Ecclesiastes 3:11,

> *He hath made every thing beautiful in his time:*
> *also he hath set the world in their heart,*
> *so that no man can find out*
> *the work that God maketh*
> *from the beginning to the end.*

"He hath set the world in the heart(s)" of many to assist with creating great works for the benefit of mankind. However it must be frustrating for those who want to know all the secrets of the Universe. We cannot and will not know it all *"from the beginning to the end."*

Earlier in September of the same that year Marconi sent his message across the Atlantic Ocean, an American inventor named King C. Gillette (1855-1932) designed the first disposable, thin, steel, safety razor blade. That year, 1901, he also founded the Gillette Safety Razor Company. His "throw-away" invention ultimately made his name and face recognized around the world. Even with his fame, life for him brought plenty of ups and downs. Living through The Great Depression, he knew both formidable success and devastating financial failure. Gillette once reflected,

Material wealth is not divisible without loss.
But knowledge is divisible to infinity...

"Knowledge is divisible to infinity." As long as mankind exists on Earth his needs will continue to evolve.

With the 1800's came the Industrial Revolution and a full scale introduction of assembly lines. That meant mass production techniques rose to new levels. "Inspired" inventions quickly picked up speed in the decades that followed. To mention a few, in the 1920's along came the Talon zipper. Designed by a Swedish-born immigrant named Otto Frederick Gideon Sundback (1880-1954), the new way to quickly fasten boots and clothes was manufactured in Meadville, Pennsylvania. It replaced the earlier, time-consuming, hookless fasteners used on shoes and boots. Today we cannot imagine life without zippers. They efficiently close nearly everything from pencil cases to freezer bags to tents to evening gowns to astronaut space suits.

In 1928, a godsend to medicine occurred when the Scottish scientist, Alexander Fleming (1881-1955), accidently discovered penicillin. (The word "accidently" was used intentionally. Fleming believed there are no accidents, only opportunities that are either recognized or ignored.) In this case Fleming definitely recognized his opportunity. That recognition heralded the modern day use of antibiotics to cure and/or control diseases. In reflection, Fleming once mused,

When I woke up just after dawn on September 28, 1928,
I certainly didn't plan to revolutionize all medicine
by discovering the world's first antibiotic,
or bacteria killer...
But I guess that was exactly what I did.

Inspirations bestowed on specifically selected individuals, such as Fleming, arrive via the mind. Sometimes they appear without any apparent effort, except that the person possesses the prior training and interest. And the individual recognizes what has come into their mind or, as in Fleming's case, sees what rests before their eyes.

Returning from an August vacation Fleming noticed one dish, among several in his cluttered laboratory table, was contaminated with a fungus. The fungus had destroyed all the staphylococci around it. Eventually that discovery became the drug penicillin. It marked the onset of modern antibiotics and eventually gave birth to the entire pharmaceutical empire.

In his work a humble Fleming cautioned young scientists to acknowledge that new discoveries often result from being aware of the opportunities that "visit them." And, he added, the mind's recognition of the usefulness in pursuing those ideas must follow. As must be the case for each of us as well.

Penicillin drugs were the first group of antibiotics discovered to effectively destroy a host of bacteria causing illnesses. Curiously, the word penicillin is a derivative of the Latin word "penicillus" which means paintbrush. As the paintbrush used to combat bacteria related issues, penicillin saved the lives of thousands of Allied servicemen during World War II. Some consider penicillin to be the most important medical discovery of the 20th Century.

"The invention that forever changed the way we write" was the ballpoint pen. Credit for its invention goes to Lasziό Birό (1899-1985), a Hungarian newspaper editor. In 1938, he designed the writing tool out of frustration. All earlier models of pens tore the paper, smudged copy, and had to be continually refilled. Eventually a man named Marcel Bich bought Birό's invention patent in 1945. It turned into the Bich Company's famous Bic pen.

The remote garage door opener became popular after World War II. Two different American designers, working with the same wartime technology used to detonate bombs, came up with ways to remotely open garage doors. Initially the new openers caused quite a stir, especially in neighborhoods where pranksters lived. All the opener frequency settings were the same. Anyone with a remote control could slowly drive along a street and open and close the garage doors of everyone who had electric door devices. I remember sitting in the kitchen of our home having dinner and hearing our garage door first go up and then back down as a friendly trickster slowly drove by merrily honking the car's horn and waving. The at-first-humorous, but could-have-turned-dicey problem quickly received modification. Today's overhead doors re-set their frequencies automatically.

The residential, riding, lawn mower made its entrance into the marketplace in the 1950's. Inventions that followed included the jumbo jet in 1969 and the mobile phone four years later.

In 1973, a man named Martin Cooper (1928-), who worked for Motorola, was gifted with the inspiration for a mobile phone. His 2½-pound, wireless, portable telephone literally dialed him into communication history and nearly killed him at the same time. In his excitement, on the first day he realized his remote phone actually worked, he dialed one of his long-time AT&T

adversaries. At the time Cooper was standing on a busy Manhattan street corner in New York City. In Cooper's distracted elation, a speeding taxi almost ran over him.

In the 20th Century, formidable original designs for bridges, cars, product packaging, and architectural structures emerged. One truly inspired visionary was the American architect R. Buckminster Fuller. It is interesting to note the future architect and structural designer had difficulties with geometry in grammar school. Later Harvard University expelled him… twice. The first expulsion came when he spent all his money partying with a vaudeville troupe. The second time they expelled him permanently for "Irresponsibility and lack of interest."

Fuller moved on to work for a while in a Canadian meatpacking plant. Eventually he experienced the biting tragedy of bankruptcy. In 1922, due to the failure of a business venture for the housing industry undertaken with his father-in-law, Fuller found himself jobless. Nearly penniless, he and his family turned to living in low income housing in Chicago. He was 32 years of age. During that time Fuller's spirits dipped to their lowest ebb. He was not only brought down by his financial disaster, but by the untimely passing of his young daughter, Alexandra. Her death, at nearly 4-years of age, devastated him. In those pre-penicillin/ pre-inoculation years, she died from the complications of polio and spinal meningitis.

After five years of heavy drinking, thoughts of suicide, and regular bouts of severe depression, Fuller finally set aside his debilitating habits and self-pitying remorse. In 1927, ennobled once again, he determined to carry on by somehow making positive differences in the lives of others around the world. He began what he called,

... an experiment, to find what
a single individual [could] contribute
to changing the world and benefiting all humanity.

Fully committed to his goal, for the rest of Fuller's life he generated inventions for the benefit of mankind.

The geodesic dome reigns as one of his hallmark creations. In 1949, at Black Mountain College in North Carolina, he constructed a spherical shape that could support its own weight. Although not the first domed structure designed, Fuller gets credit for developing the mathematics that made the construction of the round shape stronger and more suitable for uses worldwide. When the huge ball structure gained international attention in the 1950's it brought Fuller universal fame. However, throughout the productive years of his life, he modestly considered himself to be,

...the property of the universe.

His dedicated his efforts to developing low cost housing options, working with groups on global thinking, and researching renewable energy sources. All of which have benefited humanity. He referred to his efforts as,

...the property of all humanity.

Fuller's thoughts on the purpose he considered he served on Earth deserve reflective examination. Briefly summing up his perspective on his typically unassuming position he wrote,

I live on Earth at present,
and I don't know what I am.
I know that I am not a category.

I am not a thing — a noun.
I seem to be a verb,
an evolutionary process –
an integral function of the universe.

As *"an integral function of the universe,"* in Fuller's observations of the Universe, he wrote,

Everything you've learned in school as "obvious"
becomes less and less obvious
as you begin to study the universe.
For example, there are no solids in the universe.
There's not even a suggestion of a solid.
There are no absolute continuums.
There are no surfaces.
There are no straight lines.

Technically speaking, and in support of Fuller's position, truly *"there are no solids in the universe."* For that matter, there are no solids on Earth. As previously offered, the molecular energy that created the Universe is the same energy that forms everything on Earth. The vibrations of the Universe hold all the shapes we recognize together, including ourselves.

In 1970, a curious 10-year old boy wrote to Fuller. He wanted to know if Fuller considered himself a "doer" or a "thinker." The following is a portion of Fuller's reply to young Michael,

The things to do are:
the things that need doing,
that you see need to be done,
and that no one else seems
to see need to be done.

Then you will conceive
your own way of doing
that which needs to be done —
that no one else has told you to do
or how to do it.
This will bring out the real you
that often gets buried inside a character
that has acquired
a superficial array of behaviors
induced or imposed by others
on the individual.

Multitudes of great minds would echo Fuller's response to the young boy. Doing that which *"no one else seems to see needs to be done."* And, *"bring(ing) out the real you"* that is not influenced by the modes or thoughts or constraints of others.

So many have marched to the rhythms of their own conceptions. Albert Einstein, Thomas Alva Edison, Guglielmo Marconi, King C. Gillette, Otto Frederick Gideon Sundback, Laszió Biró, Alexander Fleming, Martin Cooper, and R. Buckminster Fuller. The actual list goes beyond extensive. On it, umpteen names appear. Names of men and women who saw *"the things that need(ed) doing"* and aggressively tackled their inspirations or massaged the efforts of those who went before them. Men and women whose organically shapeless, formless minds recognized and acted upon the sparks of genius they received. And our lives are all richer because of them.

The mind is an ungraspable entity with no perimeters. Its origins emanate from the vastness of the Universe. Fuller firmly acknowledged that concept. He, along with the likes of Albert Einstein and Thomas Edison, strongly believed ideas/

inspirations arrive divinely intended for single individuals to mindfully explore and share as time and mankind's needs on Earth unfurl.

Listen to the inner you, the voice that dialogues with you all the time. Difficult as it can be to accept, there are many times when the Universe brings to *only* you great moments of inspiration, in-spiriting ideas. The quality of life on planet Earth advances through all its phases on the individual merits and diligences of single persons. Group thinking is not "the norm" when it comes to inspirations.

And, the visitations of inspirational thoughts do not limit themselves to a strict category of individuals. Consider the varied backgrounds, life styles, and circumstances of the men discussed in this chapter. Fuller had a long bout with alcoholism. Carothers was a manic-depressive who committed suicide. Howe ended his days as a multi-millionaire, while Gillette went nearly bankrupt. Italy held a state funeral for Marconi when he died at the age of 63. Biro moved from Hungary to Argentina where that country's Inventors' Day is celebrated annually on his birthday, September 29th. At any moment anyone of us can receive divine "in-spiritings," inspirations. The light of dawn every morning is a miracle. So are the vast number of miracles and inspirations that come through you and to you every day of your life as you make your amazing journey. The key is to listen to the "still small voice inside" and act on the messages. Those men did. You can, too.

The uniqueness of your physical being and the inspirational miracles that come to your mind are not the only components in the world of miracles in which you live. Before exploring that vast arena, the next chapter takes a look at your intentional purpose for being on earth, your "lesson plans" for your life, your mission. Also offered are the inspired thoughts of the astronomer Carl Sagan (1934-1996) and the artist-writer Khalil Gibran (1883-1931). Two men whose pre-birth plans for their miraculous Earthly sojourns will enrich and enlighten the lives of mankind into eternity.

4

Miracles on Missions

Reflect your dreams.

In our oneness with the Universe lies the reassurance of knowing we all came to Spaceship Earth intentionally. We came with deliberate purposes. When we arrived we brought our own set of "lesson plans" complete with meticulously outlined objectives, step-by-step courses of action, and intended outcomes. By pre-birth agreements the evaluations of those plans will commence when the bell rings and "class is over." Until then, and because we enjoy freewill, we have options. We can pursue and meet the objectives of our purposes; or we can chose to do otherwise.

However, make no mistake in fancying that if you do not address your prior plans, that they will be somehow ignored. In all cases the timelines and the opportunities that go missed, ignored, or accepted, and the specific plans you committed to in your pre-birth periods, will stand. You are eternally accountable to them and for them. And, no excuses will be good enough.

At your deepest, super-conscious level you are aware that the cosmic elements of the Universe, also known as your body, are on loan to you. At the appointed hour they will be returned to their owner. They will go back to being what they have always been, which is stardust. Likewise your soul will be released to that loving Power from which you came, to that of which you have always been apart. That is the Universe, the Source, God.

To quote Fuller, again, concerning "lesson plans" and your miraculous uniqueness,

Never forget that you are one of a kind.
Never forget that if there weren't any need for you

in all your uniqueness to be on this earth,
you wouldn't be here in the first place.
And never forget,
no matter how overwhelming life's challenges
and problems seem to be,
that one person can make a difference in the world.
In fact, it is always because of one person
that all the changes that matter in the world
come about.
So be that one person.

"...it is always because of one person that all the changes that matter in the world come about. So be that one person." To make a positive difference in the world, *"be that one person"* who acts on what your miraculous mind brings to you. How empowering to realize the world has need of you and that is specifically why you are here. How amazing to also realize your ideas are totally unique to you. In the entire world, they come just to you. Recall the individuals who single-mindedly discovered penicillin, disposable razor blades, and zippers! Committees have their places, but in this Universe the power of one prevails.

A prime example of the power of one is Jesus the Christ. He was only one person preaching what he preached and doing what he did. He walked this planet for 33 years. He taught for only 3 of those years. He sent sustained tremors of faith-filled earthquakes into all time with his messages. His messages still vibrate in the hearts and minds and souls of mankind. Talk about the power of one.

I do not intend to suppose you arrived on Earth with lessons plans of the magnitude of those of Jesus, or that you possess the incites, wisdom, and powers of the Man from Nazareth. But I do know that King C. Gillette acted on his idea and surely influenced shaving for all time. By being intentionally aware Dr. Alexander Fleming unlocked the secret of the anti-biotic penicillin and millions upon millions of lives have been saved. No matter the arena, if it can be done someone can do it and that someone could be you.

How extraordinary. Each human being is created with absolutely no copies... never, ever, ever. Every single person is a bona fide miracle. And, to a person, every human being has embedded within themself the particular purposes for why they made their journey to Spaceship Earth.

On every conceivable level we are miracles. And, no matter what occurs at our physical levels, no matter how we choose to live our lives, we cannot, we do not, we are not able to totally lose touch with the Universe. We have unbreakable links to each other and eternal connections to the great Source of our being. How "out of this world" that is.

The esteemed American astronomer, Carl Sagan, advocated strong support for scientific skeptical inquiry. His research revealed a host of confirmed facts about the planets, the cosmos, and Spaceship Earth's place in the Universe. He understood the physical laws of the Universe. As a consultant and advisor to America's space program, he briefed many of the astronauts prior to their spacecraft launches. Sagan's mental acuity and industriousness contributed significantly to the study of the history of the Earth. In 1996, at a posthumous award ceremony for Dr. Sagan, one speaker said in tribute,

(His) research transformed planetary science...
his gifts to mankind were infinite.

How appropriate the gentleman speaking chose to use the

word *"infinite."* Sagan once shared this thought on science's connection to spirituality. His words circle around the word infinity and connect to the infinite life of the spirit,

"Spirit" comes from the Latin word "to breathe."
What we breathe is air,
which is certainly matter, however thin.
Despite usage to the contrary,
there is no necessary implication in the word "spiritual"
that we are talking of anything other than matter
(including the matter of which the brain is made),
or anything outside the realm of science.
On occasion, I will feel free to use the word.

Science is not only compatible with spirituality;
it is a profound source of spirituality.
When we recognize our place
in an immensity of light years
and in the passage of ages,
when we grasp the intricacy,
beauty and subtlety of life,
then that soaring feeling,
that sense of elation and humility combined,
is surely spiritual.
The notion that science and spirituality
are somehow mutually exclusive
does a disservice to both.

"...that sense of elation and humility combined" is exactly how it feels when we candidly realize the awesomeness of our place in this Universe. What a power filled statement by Sagan. In another instance Sagan wrote,

The idea that God is an oversized white male
with a flowing beard
who sits in the sky and tallies
the fall of every sparrow is ludicrous.
But if by God one means the set of physical laws
that govern the universe,
then clearly there is such a God.

Physical laws do govern the Universe. *"...such a God"* is the laws of physics and beyond. The Source reaches into the unknown, the unseen, the felt-but-not-touched, and the realm from which our minds have emanated, along with the sagacious mind of Carl Sagan. It is that realm to which our miraculous, one-of-a-kind, eternal souls will return.

For the family of Carl Sagan, when his Earth life ended, comfort came in many forms. For any whose loved ones' souls have passed to the other side, a beautiful perspective on living eternally is found in these words by the Lebanese-American, poet and artist Khalil Gibran. In his masterpiece book *The Prophet* he wrote,

You are not enclosed within your bodies,
not confined to houses or fields.
That which is you dwells above the mountain
and roves with the wind.
It is not a thing that crawls into the sun for warmth
or digs holes into darkness for safety,
But a thing free, a spirit
that envelops the earth and
moves in the ether.

Reading that lovely passage, and remembering a loved one

who has passed over, you can sense the joy of *"a thing free."* You can imagine *"a spirit that envelops the earth and moves in the ether."* A soul that *"dwells above the mountain and roves with the wind."*

In later life Sagan suffered from myelodysplasia syndrome, a condition that adversely involves the blood cells. After three, painfully unsuccessful, bone marrow transplants, he developed pneumonia. Carl Sagan passed in December of 1996. His "astronaut" life lasted only 62 years on Spaceship Earth.

Because we materialized from stardust beyond this time and planet, our bodies cannot help but vibrate with the rhythm of the Universe. Miraculously, our spiritual vibrations are eternal as well. *"…they envelop(s) the earth and move(s) in the ether."* Energy is not destroyed. The one-of-a-kind, extraordinary you will live forever. Celebrate daily the glorious everlasting miracle that is you.

As established earlier, miracles abound inside you physically, mentally, and spiritually. A dimension of miracles also exists that *comes* to you, which is *around* you. Sometimes you are aware and other times not so much. Yet miracles are not dissuaded. They continue to visit for as many reasons as there are stars in the sky. The next chapter studies miracles that are not of your design, but have been specifically designed just for you.

5

Miracles do Happen to You

Sometimes you entertain an angel.
Sometimes you are the angel.

BEYOND YOUR UNVARNISHED, SPECTACULAR, PERSONAL, miracle status, Daniel Webster defines a miracle as:

a highly improbable or extraordinary event,
a surprising development,
an astounding accomplishment,
often an occurrence with a splendid outcome

Adding to Webster's definition, it is important to remember,

Miracles arrive on their own time schedules.

Depending on who you are, where you are, and what circumstances occur with a miracle, a miracle might or might not be so splendid. For one person it could be absolutely terrific, while for someone else that same miracle could be a ghastly nightmare. This first recount of a miracle brought pleasing results for everyone.

In the book of John in *The New Testament*, the Apostle recounts the Wedding at Cana. At that ceremony, when the host realized the wine for the wedding celebration was running out, Jesus performed his first of 37 documented miracles. He turned large jugs of water into wine.

As was a common custom in biblical times, hosts served their finest wine first. After the merry-making guests drank all of it and were relaxed, the lesser quality wine was served. The hosts always assumed that none would be the wiser. At the Cana celebration, and as a result of Jesus' miracle, the well aware, albeit relaxed, guests quickly tasted the difference. They complimented the host, expressing their pleasure because they noticed he had reversed the usual procedure. The wine they were drinking, the water Jesus had turned into wine, tasted finer than what had been served to them earlier. That miracle brought about a splendid outcome. The party enjoyed a flavorful, thirst-quenching, fine-tasting wine, while the relieved host looked on with delight.

This next account is not filled with happy endings for all parties involved.

In *The Old Testament*, in the book of Exodus, the Prophet Moses describes the angry Egyptians chasing after him when he and the Israelites fled across the desert to escape their 400 years of slavery. As they approached the Red Sea, which was a natural barrier between them and freedom, the sea miraculously rolled back to allow them to cross to the opposite bank. Once the Israelites all reached the other side, the body of water swept back into its bed drowning the Egyptian soldiers who were following in lightning pursuit.

Depending on which of the banks people were standing, the miracle represented a glorious event or the height of disaster. For Moses and the Tribes of Israel it came as a tremendous relief, a true miracle. For the Pharaoh it evidenced itself as a shocking catastrophe. In utter horror he helplessly watched as the churning waters of the Red Sea claimed his best soldiers, choicest officers, finest chariots, and fastest horses.

Returning to Webster's definition, he wrote that a miracle is *"a highly improbable or extraordinary event."* The recount of the Red Sea phenomenon certainly qualifies for that definition. Skeptics, analytical wizards, and naysayers still ponder how the Red Sea rolled out and then back in its bed. They cite the phases of the moon, the position of the tides, and when all else fails they turn to the sheer improbable possibility of it at all. The speculations are many. Nonetheless somehow without boats, bridges, or inner tubes, Moses and the Israelites escaped to the opposite shore of the Red Sea and beyond the grasp of the Egyptians.

Miracles are improbable and extraordinary. They seem to unfailingly reach beyond the expected and anticipated. They frequently slant toward the paranormal. They go into the realms some people refer to as strange incidents, hallucinations, delusions, lucky breaks, inexplicable occurrences, or quirks of fate. No matter what they are called, miracles defy nature or naturally anticipated events.

In regard to a question about miracles that visit us, the early Christian theologian St. Augustine of Hippo (354-430) responded by saying,

Miracles are those times when
God walks unusual paths.

St. Augustine's insightful visualization and wisdom speaks to his depth of spirit. Additionally, what lends delight to miracles visiting us is, miracles that we know we are, we are visited by miracles more often than we acknowledge. There honestly are *"those times when God walks unusual paths."*

In fact, your entire lifetime on Spaceship Earth is wrapped up in a perpetual miracle. Miracles visit and impact you all the time. Your entire lifetime is filled with miracles. Here's an example of a miracle or what Webster would describe as *"a surprising development."*

Overwhelmed with stress and worry, an exasperated woman wandered aimlessly around in her house. Her day had dissolved into trying to cope with a serious issue over which she seemingly had no control. She was getting nothing constructive done.

Finally she got in her car and drove to a nearby mall. She hoped to occupy her mind with something else.

As she passed an office supply store she decided to park the car and go inside. Using the excuse she needed to purchase some printing products, she quickly found the aisle. Aisle A in mid-afternoon on a weekday stood completely empty. She was delighted. She wanted to be alone. She moved midway down the aisle and selected a business card packet to consider. After a few minutes she suddenly sensed she was not alone. She glanced up from the package she was casually studying and there he stood. She decided to ignore him, but sensed he was looking at her. Then she "felt" him moving closer.

He was stocky, middle aged, and needed a shave yesterday. He wore a wrinkled flannel shirt under a rumpled, down-filled, navy jacket with little white feathers peeking out here and there. His baggy pants were several inches too short, and his scuffed shoes had probably never seen a coat of polish. His overall image certainly did not appeal to her.

Her quick glance at him included noticing that he leaned on a cane. She momentarily wondered why she had not heard him approach. Or at least been aware of his shuffle to the other side of the rack. Now he stood directly in front of her. No matter, she had no intention of acknowledging him. She just hoped he would move on… and soon.

Then, he stepped even closer, and the worst happened. He spoke. "Lots of nice choices, aren't there?"

She felt compelled to recognize him. It would be rude to not reply. She decided to deliberately keep her answer short. "Yes, but I think I've found what I want," was her brisk retort.

As if he had determined she should hear it, he began telling her his story. "I'm lucky to be here," he said. "Five years ago I was a successful businessman in Kentucky. Suddenly I started getting dizzy spells. My problem was diagnosed as a fast growing tumor on my brain stem. All the specialists said I might live 6-9 months. They told me that surgery could alleviate the pain, but after the surgery I wouldn't be able to walk or talk. My wife and I began endless rounds to see specialists. We saw the very best."

"They all said the same thing, "First your balance will go, then your short-term memory. Eventually you will be unable to feed yourself or even sit alone." As if that wasn't enough, the bills began to pile up. I lost all three of my businesses."

He paused for a moment in melancholy reflection. Then he continued, "The pain intensified, and finally I had to have surgery. I was pronounced clinically dead on the operating table. Luckily for me, somehow they revived me. However, the doctors had all been right, I could not walk or talk."

"Then we lost our house. Medical costs wiped out the last of our savings. We weren't sure we would make it. Then we got word that my Dad had passed away in Pennsylvania. We had no idea that he would leave his house to us. But, he did. It was paid for, so we moved up here."

"Shortly after we got settled my wife was in a department store at a cosmetic counter. A woman came up to her. Out of the blue the lady offered her a part-time job. She had been hoping to find work, but we never expected it to happen like that. I mean, my wife finding part-time work without even having to look for it. The money she now makes covers our necessities. And, my wife still has time to be at home with me."

At first, the woman had been annoyingly skeptical of this stranger and his spontaneous story. Now she was observing him more closely. Albeit with the cane, he stood solidly in front of her. He spoke distinctly. He knew exactly what he was saying.

"With time," he continued, "my body began to fight back. The tumor just disappeared and I found I could speak. My memory is getting better day-by-day. And as you can see, I can walk now."

Then he stepped closer to her and slowly, but firmly, added, "It was our faith that pulled us through. When the troubles all started my family agreed, no matter what was going to happen, we would not lose our faith. We would be thankful for every blessing big or small. Our faith became our strength. We never gave up hope."

He paused and looked directly at her. Then in deliberately measured words he continued. "Regardless of what life brings, you have to believe. It is so important. Look at me. Look at me! Miracles do and will happen."

By now she was riveted on this stranger. Silently she felt shame for her earlier pettiness. Pettiness over what she now realized, in comparison to his story, was a trifling insignificant issue. She was acutely aware of how vitally important his story was to her.

When he finally finished, she smiled at him. Then she sincerely thanked him for sharing his story. To which he simply replied, "I looked into your eyes and I knew you would understand."

"Yes," she said, with a catch in her voice, "I really do understand."

She momentarily looked down to replace the packet she had been holding in her hands. When she looked up he was gone. The entire length of Aisle A was empty. She raced to the next aisle, quickly walked down it and then looked down the length of the one beside it. She walked across the fronts of all the other aisles, and she peered out the windows into the parking lot. The man was not to be found. He had vanished.

Where did he go? He defied "normal behavior" by disappearing into thin air. A man, who minutes earlier had stood solidly before her balancing himself with a cane, a man learning to walk again, had evaporated. How could that have happened?

The story is true. I am that woman. I remember leaving the store that afternoon without any purchases. I left mentally reeling as I tried to process how a scruffy, middle-aged stranger had walked up to me in the store, delivered a compelling message specifically tailored for me, and then totally dematerialized. Had I been visited by a miracle through that shabbily dressed man leaning on a cane? A miracle timed with a necessary message and targeted specifically for me? My answers to those questions were, "Yes."

That miracle dramatically changed my outlook that day. That miracle changed my outlook for the rest of my life. Although the man initially met with resistance from me, I will be eternally grateful that I had the patience to look at him and listen to him. In Hebrews 13:2 we are reminded to greet others with dignity and respect.

Do not neglect to show
hospitality to strangers,
for thereby
some have entertained angels unawares.

If there were no angels, God would not have mentioned them.

And if the Universe did not hold dimensions beyond what we can see with our eyes, we would have nowhere else to go when our time on Earth runs out. Perhaps you have been the recipient of an encounter similar to mine. Or perhaps the next chapter will hold special meanings for you. Miracles take many forms.

6

Miracles are Gifts

We are "on loan." What a comfort to know
we do not belong to ourselves.

ALTHOUGH WE KNOW WE CANNOT live forever, we tend to pretend there is no end. However, there are times when we probably consider what it must be like to "cross over to the other side." Here is an extraordinary account of a miracle based on that theme. It visited a couple in my community.

As life partners, they had been happily married for several decades. So, it came as an agonizing shock when they learned he had an incurable illness and only a few months to live. All their plans for a carefree retirement and a fun filled future together instantly melted away.

As his condition worsened, she stayed close to him. Eventually she kept an around-the-clock vigil at his bedside. As the end approached, she tenderly held his hand and helplessly watched as his shallow breathing slowed. Finally he sighed deeply and relaxed into eternity.

Noting he had stopped breathing, the attending nurse rushed out of the hospital room frantically calling for the staff, hoping the team could revive him. Teary-eyed, the wife watched her go. Then she turned back to her husband to wait for help to come.

As she did so he suddenly opened his eyes. And looking directly at her, he said, "I only came back to tell you something. I came back to tell you what a glorious place awaits you. I have never seen such light. Nor have I felt such pure love and peace."

Then he closed his eyes for the last time. In the distance, his wife could hear the staff rapidly approaching. However, she knew their efforts to revive him would be futile. He had stepped into eternity's light.

What an extraordinary gift he gave her when he returned to say, "…a glorious place awaits you. I have never seen such light. Nor have I felt such pure love and peace."

For her that was a miraculous unexpected revisit, a divine intervention, a clear affirmation of the power of eternal life over death. Does that impromptu return qualify as a miracle? There can be no question.

A similar experience happened to the wife of Thomas Edison. At 84 years of age, in October of 1931, in New Jersey, Thomas Edison lay in a deep diabetic coma. His faithful wife Mina sat at her vigil by his bed. Shortly before he passed, Edison abruptly awoke. Looking directly at his devoted wife, he softly said,

It is very beautiful over there…

Then Edison smiled, slowly closed his eyes, and moved on to the other side.

The two stories of those men who awoke from deep comas to speak of the other side affirm life exists in a space beyond Earth's time. Even though those events were unique to the family members who shared them, others have also known such sweetness in sorrow at the time of a loved one's passing.

I offer one last recount of a miracle, but this one takes a slightly different twist.

When my son was small he loved to spend time with my Father in his basement workshop. It was customary for them, after dinner, to tinker down there together in the evenings for several hours. My parents even bought Steve his own set of overalls "to wear to work" in the workshop.

My Dad, who years before built the house we lived in, taught Steve a lot about tools, how to use them and how to handle them safely. One tool that held particular fascination for my son was a palm-sized wood planer. Steve spent hours making mounds of wood curls. He became a master at planing pieces of scrap lumber down to shapes that resembled crude relatives of toothpicks. My Dad promised Steve that when he got older he would give him the wood planer to keep.

In the fall of 1981, after Dad had passed the previous July, my Mother took time to sort through all his tools. She chose some to keep for her own use. Some she gave to grandchildren, and others she designated for Dad's friends. She selected a few to sell, and the broken rusted ones she discarded. As she sorted she intentionally looked for the little wood planer. She never found it.

Every time my Mother went into Dad's workshop in the years that followed she never stopped glancing around. Always hopeful that some how that little wood planer might be hiding in plain sight. It never was.

Fifteen years passed. As had become Mom's custom, when she needed a hammer, a nail, or a screwdriver she went downstairs to "borrow" it from Dad's toolbox collection. One day in late autumn when she entered the workshop, resting on top of the toolbox lid she had lifted hundreds of times sat the little wood planer.

In 1981, the year his Grandfather passed, Steve had been 12 years old. Steve was 28 years old in 1996. On Christmas morning of that year one of his gifts was a small, brightly wrapped, cardboard box. Although his Grandmother had wrapped the present, no tag was attached. When he opened the box, Steve realized why no tag had been on the package. Inside he found the little wood planer. The long-ago promise had been kept.

Where had the little tool been? Since no one used the workshop, and my Mother lived alone, who put it back? How did the very same planer Steve had used 15 years earlier get on top of the lid of the toolbox? She found it in exactly the same spot where my Dad always placed it. My Mother had no answers. Except to slowly shake her head and softly say, "One day it was just there."

All the accounts I have shared are true. They really happened. All of them represent examples of the types of miracles that surround us in our daily lives.

People do have unexpected encounters with others. Often strangers deliver just the right message at exactly the right time and then are never seen again. Some people have had loved ones cross over and, if not with their words, perhaps with the aroma of cologne or the smell of motor oil or the scent of flowers, the deceased have returned to lend comfort in times least expected. Others have "re-found" lost items in obvious places, exactly where they sat many years before.

As for the miracles around you, and remembering, *"miracles arrive on their own time schedules,"* you have the capacity to recognize and interact with miracles more often than you probably acknowledge. The messages that come into your experiences arrive in a myriad of ways. One of mine was the needed-a-shave-yesterday man with a cane that I encountered in an office supply store. What is critically important to keep in mind is that it is not about who delivers the message. *It is all about the message.* Recognizing the miracles that happen and taking the time to consider the messages we receive is what is most important.

Fascinating as they are, miracles do not always involve people. The miracle that visits you could be a little bird that curiously refuses to stop pecking at your window. Or you might discover bits of colored string or coins in obvious but unusual places. Those occurrences bring into your mind exactly the reasons for which they are intended. They call forth the gentle, supportive, comforting thoughts of a loved one. Perhaps you have sensed the energy of someone who reached back from eternity, with a sensation of warmth and assurance. Maybe, like my Mother, you found a long lost item that no amount of searching had produced.

Our lives hold so much more than what we see when we look into a mirror. We are literally surrounded by miracles. Miracles visit us all the time. They really do. On this topic, George Bernard Shaw (1856-1950), the famous Irishman, who founded the London School of Economics and wrote at least 60 plays, once said,

Miracles,
in the sense of phenomena we cannot explain,
surround us on every hand:
life itself is the miracle of miracles.

"Life itself is the miracle of miracles." Everything about your life is a miracle. Do miracles happen to you? Do they come to you in unusual ways? Are they real phenomena on this journey we call life? Absolutely. Our choice is to dismissively ignore them or honor them. Either way they are what they are. And, they "are."

For skeptics, it helps to keep in mind that miracles are not contrary to nature. But they are contrary to what we *know* about nature. One skeptical argument postulates that miracles are not based on common sense, so how can they "be." Of course they are not based on common sense, they are not common. Those who chose to not accept miracles because they need "proof" do not dilute or destroy the presence or power of miracles with negative pontifications. Disbelief does not equate to truth. To quote *The Holy Bible's* book of Ecclesiastes 3:11 (again),

He has made everything beautiful
in its time.

He has also set eternity in the human heart;
yet no one can fathom
what God has done
from beginning to end.

By grand design, our experiences and environments limit our senses of all the Universe holds. "*...no one can fathom what God has done from beginning to end.*" Man's common sense makes no sense when it comes to the awesome workings of God.

Consider the great minds mentioned in this book. Many believed that their discoveries came to them as miraculous inspirations, as Edison attested,

I am a channel,
not the originator.

Miracles are nonfiction. They are authentic Earth time experiences. Therefore, it is unreasonable to consider miracles to be hallucinations or accidents. They are as absolute as the creation of the Universe. Miracles "are." Just as we "are." After all, we walk around using minds that no one has ever seen. The obstructions rest in the limitations of our understandings, not in the validity of miracles.

As Earth bound creatures, we have no choice but to view the world through our own experiential backgrounds. If we do not know about it and have never seen it and do not understand it, then how can it be? Keep in mind that at one time the world was thought to be flat. Sailing out to far would cause a ship to go over the edge.

To be fair to all of us, we can only work with the information we have. We judge and see the world through our own lens of logic, with our own sets of beliefs. What should be remembered is that God does not.

We have lived for billions of years and we will live for billions more. We are here in this time and space by preordained design. As Dr. Fleming, who discovered penicillin understood, nothing is an accident. None of us are accidents. The Universe knows you are here, and the Universe knows why.

Throw your arms wide open and allow yourself to be wrapped in all the wonders life holds for you. Miracles do happen. You are one.

7

The Breath of God

From first inhale to last exhale
the circle of life is a miraculous cycle.

IN JULY OF 1887, IN a rural village near the town of Vitebsk in Russia's Belarus, the famous 20th Century artist, Marc Chagall (1887-1985), was born... dead. His dismayed family stared in silent shock at the tiny lifeless form. Then someone suddenly picked the newborn up by his feet and plunged him headfirst into a pail of icy water. When they quickly pulled him back out of the pail, he emerged with a loud wail. Chagall's long, creatively productive life on Earth officially started as a result of the shock of his first dunking and consequently his first breath.

In Hebrew (and in Latin, as Carl Sagan reminded us), the word for "to breathe" is the same as the word for "spirit." Exactly like Chagall, you "officially" commenced your physical life on earth with a first breath, the breath of life, the breath of the spirit. Although chances are good your earthly beginning did not start with a swift dunk head first into a pail of icy water.

Your physical body was formed before birth. However, until you breathed you could not function on this planet. As with Marc Chagall, the first breath you breathed enabled your body to live independently. It ignited your spirit.

The physical unions of men and women create human beings. But, their unions cannot genetically develop souls in those bodies. Over decades assiduous scientists and researchers have attempted to clone animals, hoping to ultimately reproduce a human in a laboratory. Eventually they might be able to create the body of a human being. However, the re-creation of a human soul is beyond their abilities. And, each of us has a soul. Each of us *is* a soul.

Considered to have been one of the intellectual literary giants of the 20th Century, the Irish writer, C. S. Lewis (1898-1963) is thought to have once said,

You don't have a soul.
You are a soul.
You have a body.

Although the exact source is debatable, since he was a Christian Apologist that could have easily been Lewis' quote. However, the message in the quote is not debatable.

Lewis authored 30 books and is revered for his fantasy threaded *The Chronicles of Narnia*, which is a series of seven novels for children. The books contain both Christian topics and ideas. During WW II, Lewis broadcast Christian-themed radio programs. They brought him wide attention, as did the explanations of his spiritual beliefs based on his platforms of logic and philosophy, hence his Christian Apologist status. Here are a few of his thoughts:

A man can no more diminish God's glory
by refusing to worship Him
than a lunatic can put out the sun
by scribbling the word,
"darkness" on the walls of his cell.

Can a mortal ask questions which
God finds unanswerable?
Quite easily, I should think.
All nonsense questions are unanswerable.

Humans are amphibians...
half spirit and half animal.
As spirits they belong to the eternal world,
but as animals they inhabit time.

In the last quote, Lewis makes a well-reasoned, Christian Apologist separation between the body and the soul. He uses the word spirit. The words "spirit" and "soul" continue to engage groups in on-going debates. The two words raise questions among language purists, theological leaders, and intellectual conceptualists. I cannot be convinced the two words deserve such heavy dialogue. They both reflect the power of God's presence in the lives of mankind. Both refer to nebulous invisible energies. For easier reading I will apply whichever term I feel best suits the information being presented.

Like our minds, our souls are within us. They are also formless and beyond medical technology's abilities to x-ray or scan. However, it is the position of most that unlike the mind, the soul is not *of* us. We need the services of our minds only while we are on Earth, while all that is embedded in us is in our souls. The soul is a component of eternity. It *"belongs to the eternal world."*

Like love, the soul is a part of God, a part of that vastness from which we have all come. Your soul is bonded to your forever self, a permanent attachment to the Universe. And, as the Universe is completely beyond man's destructive capabilities, so is your soul. Again, I say you are immortal.

Those who spend their professional lives in the arenas of science and medicine are sometimes reticent to believe in higher powers and/or immortality. Here is a surprising story about an avowed atheist. It concerns a doctor who experienced an encounter with immortality on a level he would have never expected or manufactured.

On November 8, 2008, Dr. Eben Alexander (1953-) confidently went about his usual regimen of daily activities. Diagnosing and treating issues for his patients, he depended entirely and confidently on medical science. As a highly trained and well-respected neurosurgeon, all his research had proved to him there could be no God, no soul, and certainly no heaven or life after death. Alexander's confidence rested entirely on medical science, of which he knew a great deal. He could reconcile nothing else.

On November 9th, Dr. Alexander awoke with a splitting, totally debilitating headache. Within hours he was in a hospital bed in a meningitis-induced coma. Curiously, his brain had mysteriously filled with the life-threatening E. coli bacteria. He lay in that coma for 7 days. All hope for his recovery appeared beyond possibility. Then, as the attending doctors were just about to pull all his life support systems, he suddenly awoke. His professional colleagues were at first startled and then delighted.

However, Alexander reported an unusual experience to them that occurred while he was unconscious. He contended that during the duration of his coma, he had mentally travelled to a timeless place of perfect joy and beauty. In his words,

> *...complete with angels, clouds,*
> *and departed relatives,*
> *but also including butterflies*
> *and a beautiful girl in peasant dress.*

It would be later that the mystery of the peasant-dressed girl would unravel. Alexander would learn the girl was his deceased younger sister, Betsy. Born to an unwed mother in 1953, Eben had been placed for adoption. Some time after his adoption, his biological parents married. Betsy was the daughter of his birth parents. She was his sister. She had died several years prior to Alexander's coma experience. He knew nothing about her. They had never met. A photograph later confirmed she had been the girl in the peasant dress.

Consequently due to his first-hand experiences while in the week-long coma, Alexander realized that consciousness is independent of the organic brain. As discussed in Chapter 2 of this book, the brain is not the mind. According to Alexander, medical science's current position about, and understanding of, the mind,

...now lies broken at our feet.

And, continuing,

What happened to me destroyed it,
and I intend to spend the rest of my life
investigating the true nature of consciousness
and
making the fact that we are more, much more,
than our physical brains
as clear as I can,
both to my fellow scientists
and to people at large.

In 2012, Alexander's story was published in his best-selling book *Proof of Heaven: A Neurosurgeon's Journey into the Afterlife.* In the book he maintains that death is an illusion, that an eternity of unparalleled grandeur awaits us beyond the grave. That,

Consciousness exists independent of the brain.
Consciousness is the most
profound mystery in the universe.

As he expected, turbulent criticism from within Alexander's professional ranks continues to prevail. However, the primary complaint from skeptics is that his information is "alarmingly unscientific." The real question, to me, seems to be... How can consciousness, the mind, or the soul be "scientific" when none are physical, see-able, or concrete? Alexander's critics do get one part of their complaint correct. Consciousness, the soul, and the mind are "unscientific." They are beyond the realm of science.

As Alexander learned through experience a larger dimension of the Universe does exist. And, to paraphrase Ecclesiastes 3:11, mankind's ability to understand and control everything on Earth is not an option. Some things are of God and beyond "scientific" grounding. Many of the mysteries of the Universe will continue as long as Spaceship Earth orbits the mother ship Sun.

As previously noted, our brains and our bodies are not our minds and our souls. By intentional design, the soul of a man cannot be studied under a microscope. All the answers to skeptics' questions and concerns are (quite literally) one breath away.

As with Marc Chagall, when your first breath entered your body you received the necessary energy, and your spirit accepted the opportunity, to become all you can become on this planet. With that ignited spirit you acquired all you needed to realize your mission. That breath gave you the start to work on the pre-determined set of lesson plans for your life.

One spirit's ignition gave the world Madame Marie Sklodowska Curie (1867-1934), the first woman awarded the Nobel Prize. That honor recognized her research in radioactivity, a term first coined by her and her husband, Pierre. Specifically her efforts led to the discovery of polonium and radium. In 1903, Curie and her husband shared a Nobel Prize for their work in physical science with Henri Becquerel. The three had collaborated on a research project in radiation.

In 1911, she was the sole recipient of the Nobel Prize for her research in the field of chemistry. Curie and her husband also pioneered the development of x-rays. Although she became a French citizen, she was forever proud of her Polish heritage. The chemical element polonium is named for her country. None can dispute that Madame Curie came to Spaceship Earth with quite a formidable set of lesson plans!

Unfortunately, Curie knew little about the long-lasting effects of exposure to radiation. She customarily walked around the laboratory with test tubes of radioactive isotopes in her lab coat pocket. In 1934, Madame Curie died at the age of 67 of aplastic anemia. A disease caused by her many years of working in close proximity to radiation.

Another spirit's first breath ignited the life and purposes of perhaps the most versatile athlete of the 20th Century, Olympic star, Jim Thorpe (1888-1953). The son of Native American and European ancestors, his Indian name is Wa-Tho-Huk. When translated into English the name means "Bright Path." And, Bright Path he was. Thorpe maintained the bright path of his athletic career until he was 41-years of age.

During the 1912 Olympics in Stockholm, Thorpe easily surpassed his competition in both the decathlon and the pentathlon events. He set records that stood for decades. When King Gustav V of Sweden presented Thorpe with his medals he called him,

...the greatest athlete in the world.

To which the unassumingly humble Jim Thorpe simply accepted his medals and softly replied,

Thanks, King.

Another ignition of life became the astute-beyond-astute, English writer William Shakespeare (1564-1616). As Albert Einstein is to mathematics and physics, so is William Shakespeare to the English language as a writer and dramatist. His ever-popular, intriguing, insightful works capture all our human emotions and lay open the wounds of all our conflicts. Some of his quotes have engrained themselves into society's fabric to the extent that we forget Shakespeare was the man who first penned them. Ones such as:

This above all; to thine own self be true.

To be, or not to be, that is the question.

A fool thinks himself to be wise,
but a wise man knows himself to be a fool.

To have written with such universal significance and uncomplicated truth marks Shakespeare as one of the most extraordinary writers who ever lived. His name is synonymous with the finest in literature. What an awesome lesson plan he created for himself!

Another spirit's first breath brought life to a child whose Austrian parents named him Wolfgang Amadeus Mozart (1756-1791). In his brief lifetime Mozart would compose some of the world's most beautiful classical music. He began performing at the age of 5. And, before he died at the age of 35, Mozart had refined the musical forms of the symphony, the string ensemble, and the concerto. History remembers him as one of Western civilization's most important composers.

Marc Chagall, a naturalized French citizen, worked on his imaginative artistic creations until the day he died at the age of 98. Living as long as he did, he faced quite challenging political times in the Earth's history. He experienced the horrifying years of two world wars. During the early years of World War II, he was living in southern France with his wife and daughter when the Nazi's marched into Paris. As Jews they faced sure danger. To avoid being sent to concentration camps, they escaped in the dead of night over the Pyrenees Mountains to Portugal and sought asylum in the United States. On the same day that their ship set sail for the United States, the invading Germans were in the act of devastating his entire village of Vitebsk in Belarus.

In 1947, Chagall rejoiced with the establishment of the State of Israel. He designed 12 stained glass windows for a Jerusalem hospital to honor the 12 Tribes of Israel. Although an Orthodox Jew, when he died his wife followed his wishes and located a Christian gravesite near their home in St. Paul de'Vence, France. Chagall had asked that his commitment service be both quiet and non-public. As the simple service concluded, an uninvited man no one had ever seen before stepped from behind a tree grove. He moved to the casket and softly recited the Kaddish. After he finished the last rites of the Jewish faith over Chagall's coffin, he stepped back behind the trees and was never seen again.

Some souls stay for only a few hours, a few days, or for a limited number of years like Wolfgang Mozart, who lived for only 35 years. Some race the tracks of life at high speed, laughing and singing and dancing to the very end. Others walk quieter paths, preferring the softness of dawn and dusk to the bright light of the midday sun. As no two of us are alike, so no two Earth time adventures are the same.

You did not arrive on this planet to be like anyone but yourself. Your lesson plans are your own, as are your life's experiences. Deep within your uniqueness rests the innate knowledge of your predetermined mission, your soul's personal purpose.

With all your uniqueness, make no mistake, it definitely matters where and when you were born. The country you live in, the time and date of your birth, and your biological family are no accidents. They are critical to your growth and learning and the execution of your purposes. All those givens play into the Pathways of your life's destiny. They influence the palette of adventures from which you choose your colors.

Continually relish all there is to honor about yourself. You are an astronaut/space traveler and you understand why. You are made from stardust. You are over billions of years old. You have your own handwriting style, physical body system, mind, and soul. You are an extraordinary, one-of-a-kind, remarkable miracle.

You journey through your lifetime with a decidedly personal spiritual energy that binds you to your God, your Source, and your Universe. It is that never-ending energy which perpetuates your soul. And, it gives you the breath to sustain your body during your time on Earth.

Every moment you spend on Spaceship Earth holds unprecedented possibilities, occasions, and adventures. Delightful opportunities await you. No matter at what stage of life you are in, no matter how old or young, no matter how successful or struggling, no matter where you live, or what your plans are for tomorrow… you are a miracle of the highest order.

We are many from a greater whole. We are many from one.

We came from the same place and to that same Universal Power we are destined to return. Nothing will change that. We breathe the sacred breath of life. We are living souls and therefore totally indestructible. We "are" and will "be" forever. By supernatural design we cannot be destroyed. We are immortal.

Only one breath prevents us from appreciating and understanding the whole picture. That is the breath of the spirit, the breath of God. On the other side of just one breath we will all know everything.

Be filled with gratitude for all the miracles that surround you, all the miracles that come to you, all the miracles that are tailor-made just for you, and the breath of God that sustains you. Honor the miracle that you are.

8

It is All About Joy

Enjoy. Cause joy.
It comes back to you.

HISTORIANS QUIPPINGLY ESTIMATE THE ANCIENT Egyptians spent more time and energy in life making preparations to die than they spent in life focused on living. They planned their own funeral celebrations, the interiors of their tombs, and what would go with them into the tombs. All the established rituals occupied countless hours and the efforts of large teams of people. In some instances, royals even selected *who* would go with them into their tombs.

The Egyptians believed every person had a soul/spirit, which they called "akh." After death akh would exit and re-enter the physical body at will. So they refined the practice of mummification to preserve the house of the soul... the body. Upon death, embalmers removed all the fluids and organs except the heart. To them the heart held all the records of the deceased's life on Earth.

Eventually the heart was weighed against a feather. It was called the feather of truth. The weighing occurred in front of their God Osiris. He promised eternal life to those he deemed morally worthy. Worn by the Goddess Ma'at (pronounced Ma-yet), the feather represented order, law, morality, justice, balance, and truth. Since their culture held deep-seated convictions concerning holiness and unity as they related to life on Earth and the cosmos, the scales had to balance. No heavy, immoral, or dark hearts gained permission to enter the afterlife. How fascinating. Even in the dawning years of civilization the Egyptians clearly understood the power of the soul to live eternally, as in fact it does.

At some point during the 40 days of the traditional mummification procedure, and after the weighing of the heart, the deceased would be asked two questions. The first question was,

Did you find joy?

And the second question was,

Did you give joy?

Undeniably finding and giving joy carried substantial weight, given all the deceased were only asked those two questions. And both pertained to joy.

The Egyptians believed joy to be the cornerstone to the quality of life on Earth. On several occasions, *The Old Testament's* book of Ecclesiastes speaks of joy. Known as "The Preacher's" book, it was written approximately three centuries before the birth of Jesus as a guide to living successfully and with joy. It has greatly influenced the development of Western literature. And, the ancient Egyptians would have concurred with many of its messages.

On the topic of books in *The Holy Bible*, and specifically Ecclesiastics, the American writer, Thomas Wolfe (1900-1938), once wrote,

Ecclesiastes is the greatest single piece of writing
I have ever known,
and the wisdom expressed in it
the most lasting and profound.

Wolfe is considered by many to be the foremost American novelist of the 1st half of the 20th Century. Therefore, his evaluation of *The Old Testament* book is noteworthy. Many of the verses in Ecclesiastes read like a recipe for enjoying a good life. Although the book contains cautions, its beautiful thoughts are written in a splendid descriptive prose. In support of an earlier chapter in this book on the return of the body to the stardust from which it was made and the return of the soul to its original home, Ecclesiastes 12:7 reads,

Then shall the dust return to the earth
as it was:
and the spirit shall return unto God
who gave it.

Also, an example on the topic of joy that is found in Ecclesiastes 8:15 reads,

So I commend the enjoyment of life,
because nothing is better for a man under the sun
than to eat and drink and be glad.
Then joy will accompany him in his work
all the days of the life
God has given him under the sun.

"*...the enjoyment of life*" is whole-heartedly supported in that lovely passage.

The New Testament also addresses the subject of joy many times. In the book of Romans there is a letter the Apostle Paul wrote to the Christians in the city of Rome. That letter expresses many of Paul's most clearly defined thoughts on Christian theology. It should be noted that Paul wrote his letter to the Roman followers of Christ before the great fire of Rome in 64.

An important aside is that the full-scale persecution of Rome's

Christians commenced when Nero (37-68 AD) needed scapegoats and an excuse for why Rome burned for three days. Prior to the great fire, Nero persecuted Christians on a more limited basis. For example, on special occasions he ordered groups of them rounded up and brought to his palace to be used as human torches to light his gardens in the evenings. Years before Nero's sweeping inhumane treatment of his own citizens, Paul had written to the church members in Rome encouraging them to be filled with joy. In Romans 15:13 he wrote,

May the God of hope fill you with all joy
and peace as you trust in him,
so that you may overflow with hope
by the power of the Holy Spirit.

Paul encouraged his believers to be filled *"with all joy,"* which is a powerful gift from the Spirit of God.

In sharp contrast to Nero, the Emperor Marcus Aurelius (121-189 AD) is considered to be one of the most respected Roman emperors in history. Aurelius ruled from 161-180 AD as the last of the "Five Good Emperors" of the ancient Roman Empire. Aurelius is one of the most significant of the Stoic philosophers. (Stoic philosophy focuses on reason, self-restraint, and fate.) During his lifetime, Aurelius wrote a series of 12 books. He called the collection *My Self.* Conceivably he penned them for his own private guidance, or as a diary, or a collection of his personal thoughts. They were never intended for the public in general. However, today they are widely read and quoted. They are now referred to as *Meditations.* Included in his writings are wise and succinct statements. Offered here are a few:

He who lives in harmony with himself
lives in harmony with the universe.

To live happily is an inward
power of the soul.

Very little is needed to make a happy life;
it is all within yourself,
in your way of thinking.

Marcus Aurelius centered a number of his entries on uplifting thoughts. With all the pressures of his position, it is refreshing to know that he sought *"a happy life"* for himself. He understood the important role joy played in that objective.

Appropriately nicknamed the "Philosopher King," among his writings this quote about beginning the day with joy is offered,

When you arise in the morning,
think of what a precious privilege it is to be alive…
to breathe, to think,
to enjoy, to love.

Marcus Aurelius considered morning critical to setting the stage for his day. He saw morning, when everything is renewed and fresh, as a perfect time to nourish his soul. It appears he dined on a calorie-free breakfast of thanksgiving thoughts filled with joy and love.

Earlier in the 1st Century, Jesus of Nazareth, in the final week of his life on Earth, emphasized to his 12 Disciples that joy underpinned all he had taught them. The disciple John recorded his esteemed Teacher's words in John 15:10-11.

If you keep my commands,
you will remain in my love,
just as I have kept my Father's commands

and remain in his love.
I have told you this so that my joy may be in you
and that your joy may be complete.

Jesus said, "*...that my joy may be in you...*" to remind his Disciples that joy is a "gift" bestowed upon mankind by the Creator of life. Joy is received. Joy cannot be "bought."

Thomas A. Sweet, Pastor of Market Square Presbyterian Church in Harrisburg, Pennsylvania described joy this way,

Joy is not a commodity
that can be bought or sold.
It is not a quality that can be conjured up
or worked up or manufactured.
It is not even (as we sometimes think)
the result of favorable circumstances in our lives.
Joy is embedded
in the fabric of life itself
awaiting our awaking to it,
our discovery of it,
our trust in it.
Joy is God's great desire for us.

We arrive with joy *"embedded in the fabric of life itself."* If anyone should question that perspective, do a quick study of little children. Aside from their "physical-need alerts," joy is their first emotion. Children are synonymous with purity, innocence, exuberance, enchantment, and a natural spirituality. We have all been children, the joy we knew in those years is still with us. Joy never leaves. We carry it in our hearts all our lives, even when times and circumstances cloud its passion. Joy remains an emotion that undergirds us and reminds us, like Jesus reminded

The Twelve, that we belong. We can always rest joyfully in the arms of God. Joy, like love, intertwines with the soul. It stands to reason we would bring it to our Earth time experiences. Joy serves as a Pathway to uniting us with the Source.

The passion joy carries layers of emotional ups and downs. Some times joy brings overflowing pleasure. Other times, because we have known great joy, it generates circumstances that are sorrowful and/or uncomfortable. On the dichotomy of the topic of joy, Khalil Gibran wrote in his book *The Prophet,*

When you are joyous, look deep into your heart
and you shall find it is only that
which has given you sorrow
that is giving you joy.
When you are sorrowful look again in your heart,
and you shall see that in truth
you are weeping for
that which has been your delight.

As an artist, writer, and the 3rd best selling poet of all time, Gibran's message cautions us. The heights of joy we can experience are in direct balance to the depths of sorrow we can endure.

In my frame of reference, emotions are akin to a teeter-totter. The fuller and more openly you live your life the richer and higher your joys. Keeping in mind that in those times when you are sky high on joy, the other end of the teeter-totter is resting on the ground. Therefore, when the intensity of your sorrow is deep, the end of the seesaw you are sitting on is resting at the ground. Again, quoting Gibran,

Some of you say, "Joy is greater than sorrow,"
and others say, "Nay, sorrow is the greater."

But I say unto you, they are inseparable.
Together they come,
and when one sits alone with you at your board,
remember that the other is asleep upon your bed.
Verily you are suspended like scales
between your sorrow and your joy.
Only when you are empty
are you at standstill and balanced.

"Only when you are empty" are you without emotion, without joy, without sorrow, even alienated from the Source. With joy in your heart you cannot be empty, estranged, or *"at (a) standstill."*

Even in life's darkest hours when you are struggling emotionally, spiritually, and mentally your soul innately trusts the God to whom you belong. In that knowledge and love can rest your strength and oneness. To seek and acknowledge joy in every circumstance draws you closer to the Source, to your God, to your Universe.

Like Gibran, Sweet spoke of joy's dichotomy as,

Joy is not, as we sometimes imagine,
the fruit of good fortune and pleasant living,
but rather the acceptance of the full mix of life,
trusting that all of it is being
lived in God
in whom our lives are kept.
Anyone can feel sunny
when things are going well
but joy undergirds us in the hard,
difficult, and disappointing times as well.
...we trust that not even
the dark and desperate things

will overwhelm us or
undo us but teach us and
make us more human.

Joy will not abandon us, but rather *"teach us and make us more human."* As we walk the sunlit paths and/or as we stumble in the darkness, *"joy undergirds us."* The French Jesuit visionary and philosopher, Pierre Teilhard de Chardin once succinctly penned,

Joy is the infallible sign
of the presence of God.

As a gift of the spirit and a permanent part of the soul, joy is an emotion like none other. Joy is a *"sign of the presence of God,"* an eternal presence that stays with us always and in all ways.

From the ancient Egyptians to Jesus of Nazareth in the 1st Millennium, and from the writings of Marcus Aurelius to Thomas Wolfe, and onto the futuristic 21st Century, the message has never wavered. Joy is embedded in your soul. As an elation that reflects the highest feelings of happiness, exuberance, bliss, and abundance, it connects to your higher self.

Given the choice, surely every person wants to be joy filled. Everyone wants be pleased with the quality of life and the circumstances that surround them. At the close of your time on Earth how will/would you answer the two questions?

Did you find joy?
Did you give joy?

9

Choose to be Joy Filled

Joy in your soul is nutrition for your heart.

IF POSSIBLE, DEDICATE YOURSELF TO maintaining a wholesome balance physically, mentally, emotionally, spiritually, and socially. Although there will be times when that can be a tough slough, it is a worthy rewarding goal. Having your life in balance guarantees favorable chances you will enjoy all the plentiful-ness life has to offer. Underpinning the five umbrella headings of physical, mental, emotional, spiritual, and social one extremely pivotal word hangs. That word is "joy." Happy, elated, exuberant, buoyant, sunny, blissful, contented, cheerful, glad... those adjectives all connect to the power filled word JOY. Joy welds substantial sway over the well-balanced states of each of us.

As a rule all societies tend to view "enjoying life" as a paramount goal. It definitely is an admirable and intentional aspiration toward which to aim. Researchers have discovered that individuals who think joy filled cheerful thoughts live longer. Given ordinary conditions, and excluding accidental deaths, their studies affirm that happy people live 14% longer, as in 7.5 to 10 years longer than their pessimistic counterparts.

Optimists routinely exhibit lower blood pressure readings and experience fewer incidences of acute cardiovascular diseases. Upbeat thinkers benefit from higher energy levels. Because of their innate resiliency they manifest healthier physical and psychological conditions. The bodies of physically active people generate endorphins that produce feelings of well being. The endorphins permeate the whole of the person. While optimistic people generate their own endorphins, during acupuncture procedures technicians often insert needles at anatomy points to trigger the production of endorphins in the bodies of their patients. That is done to encourage pleasurable feelings after treatments.

Optimists also cope with stress and hardships more appropriately. Their general patterns are to objectively recognize what comes to them. Then they usually opt to constructively consider the circumstances and then move forward more swiftly then pessimists. They deliberately choose to focus their attentions on positives. Even if those positives are small aspects, mini-pluses, or barely viable potentials. In contrast to pessimists, they rarely dither over pocket-sized nagging issues, nor are they overwhelmed forever by massive catastrophes. As an example: In the aftermath of a disaster such as a flood, an earthquake, or a fire, optimists will focus on what remains that is good. They will not squander large amounts of their energy or time lamenting over what they no longer have.

Additionally, those with cheerful personalities exhibit a broader range of emotions than their sullen, morose, resentful counterparts. Optimistic folks do get depressed, sad, and miserable. A full emotional range is "normal" and mentally healthy. But statistics have proven that optimists spend three times more time being positive than their pessimistic opposites. Moreover pessimists are inclined to turn inward and obsess with their miseries in private. Optimists willingly move on. They engage themselves with others in social environments. They stay active, maintain a circle of positive-outlooking friends, and do not waste their time consumed with anxieties, tensions, or worries.

Positive people display a natural sense of freedom and adventure about themselves. They relish new exposures and experiences, while gratefully savoring the small treats that come they ways just as much. They exude confidence. They represent an active group that "gets things done."

The predisposition in this chapter is to not overtly dwell on the negative pessimistic aspects of personalities. However a few points warrant sharing. Individuals with negative tendencies, attitudes, and debasing thoughts manifest lower energy vibration levels than their counterparts. They suffer more frequently from physical ailments such as high blood pressure and severe arthritis. They tend to contract higher rates of life threatening systemic diseases and illnesses such as cancer and heart-related conditions. They habitually do not "feel" healthy. Yet they never seem to know exactly why. Studies show that pessimists tire more readily. They often "drag their feet," unable to get projects done promptly or efficiently. Forces without and within drain them. Those forces could ultimately destroy them and (as research has shown) consume them.

To pessimists, the lives of optimists appear fuller. Jealous skeptics often assume "those lucky optimists" enjoy uninterrupted prosperous lives with little or no effort. Actually positive folks really do "work at it." Thus, optimists intentionally live richer fuller lives. That does not mean positive thinkers are automatically money-richer, as in "get happy, get rich." It means optimists' lives are richer with intriguingly stimulating experiences, richer in fruitful productivity, and richer with the benefits of good health and joy. That is how positive people see their lives. That is how they live.

The esteemed Irish writer and poet, Oscar Wilde (1854-1900) made a clever contrast between the perspectives of optimists and pessimists in his play *Lady Windermere's Fan.* In the best-remembered line from that comedy he wrote,

We are all in the gutter,
but some of us are looking at the stars.

From the gutter, pessimists would fret about a torrential rain coming and drowning them in a sea of mud. From the gutter, optimists would be *"looking at the stars"* where they would want to be, where they would be determined to go. The ambitious optimists would not be *in* the gutter when the rain started. If it ever did. Optimists look up, not down.

On the topic of looking up, the silent film star and renowned, British, comedian Charlie Chaplin (1889-1977) once said,

You'll never find a rainbow
if you are always looking down.

Chaplin learned about looking up from cruel first-hand experience. As a child he knew only poverty and deprivation. Born into an unstable family in 1889, later his destitute mother had no choice but to send him and his older brother to live in a London workhouse. Charlie was only 7-years old. In his teens, his mother died from physical neglect as a result of her chronic bouts with insanity. His father followed not long after, dying from cirrhosis of the liver brought on by his acute alcoholism.

At a young age Chaplin took advantage of his natural acting talents to support himself by working in the vaudeville circuit. With the introduction of silent films, he moved into that realm. He eventually became an actor, producer, screenwriter, and director.

However, his entire life was akin to a plaster horse on a carrousel. Colorfully painted and exciting he went up and down and around and around never staying in one space for any length of time. Over the years he was divorced three times. He suffered the accusations of being a communist sympathizer. He battled false paternity suit charges. He watched as his film projects ebbed and flowed with the whims of the public and the fickle press. Yet, Chaplin never gave up.

His concocted image of himself as The Tramp is iconic in film history, as are the 75 years that he dedicated to the silver screen. Without Chaplin's eternal optimism in the face of horrific odds the world would have been a little less joy filled. In spite of all Chaplin battled, he made people laugh. Charlie Chaplin always chose joy.

Another Brit with grit, and remembered as one of the greatest wartime leaders of the 20th Century, was Britain's Prime Minister, Sir Winston Churchill (1874-1965). He once observed what he considered the basic differences between optimists and pessimists when he said,

A pessimist
sees the difficulty in every opportunity;
an optimist
sees the opportunity in every difficulty.

Churchill's astute remark defined his personal philosophy, which was to always look beyond the difficulty and see the opportunity the difficulty presented. Involved in British politics for fifty years, his positive, powerful, public persona served him and his nation well time and time again. In all of Britain's history he ranks as one of its most influential leaders. Churchill's resolve during World War II to never consider defeat inspired his countrymen to be even greater than they thought they could be.

He was famous for his candid inspiring rhetoric. Shortly after he accepted the position of Prime Minister of the United Kingdom in 1940, he is remembered for saying,

... we shall fight in France,
we shall fight on the seas and oceans,
we shall fight with growing confidence
and growing strength in the air,
we shall defend our island,
whatever the cost may be,
we shall fight on the beaches,
we shall fight on the landing grounds,
we shall fight in the fields and in the streets,
we shall fight in the hills;
we shall never surrender.

"We shall never surrender" became Britain's battle cry. Make no mistake, England greatly suffered from the brutal ravages of the Nazi bombing raids. The lack of supplies and the utter destitutions of war gave rise to merciless living conditions at home. Churchill suffered with his countrymen, but remained defiantly strong and firmly at the helm. Consequently, privately he battled clinical depression from it all. Nevertheless, he steeled himself with a determined resolve in the face of his citizenry. He realized the higher goal was to save his nation. The Brits, in turn, were energized and motivated. Along with The Allies, they eventually secured a victory over Hitler's Nazi Germany. They never even considered surrendering.

The history of the world has given us many examples of "optimism under fire" to admire and from which to learn. If you look, you will find that children's books also hold insightful examples of the differences between optimists and pessimists. A lovely, little, three sentence dialogue in *Winnie the Pooh*, points out the positive frame of mind of little Pooh Bear. Written by the author A.A. Milne (1882-1956), it goes like this,

"What day is it?"
It's today," squeaked Piglet.
"My favorite day," said Pooh.

Concurring with the eternal optimist Pooh Bear would have been the American lecturer and writer Ralph Waldo Emerson (1803-1882). He once wrote,

Write it on your heart that
every day is the best day in the year.

Emerson strongly advocated for enriching the soul with joy. He believed the euphoria that it brings to the individual is essential to a wholesome life. He considered all things on Earth to be connected to God and therefore divine. As an avowed optimist, Emerson was convinced about the goodness of human nature and the goodness of the Universe as a whole. Understandably he, like Marcus Aurelius and Pooh Bear, would consider *"every day is the best day"* and so it is.

In another passage from *Winnie the Pooh,* Milne wrote,

"It's snowing still," said Eeyore (the donkey) *gloomily.*
"So it is." (Pooh said)
"And freezing."
"Is it?"
"Yes," said Eeyore.
"However," he (Pooh) *said, brightening up a little,*
"we haven't had an earthquake lately."

What a refreshingly crisp, uncomplicated dialogue. Milne lightheartedly illustrated through his charming little characters a positive way to look at a wintry day. But it could be a dialogue adaptable to any issue.

Churchill knew well that how we perceive things to be is exactly how they are to us. And, therefore, how they will often seem to others. We periodically forget how our outlooks affect the emotions, attitudes, and responses of those around us.

To bring closure to this topic on optimism versus pessimism, we can always count on the Irish literary critic and writer, George Bernard Shaw. He predictably and humorously put optimism and pessimism in to a simple perspective when he wrote,

Both optimists and pessimists contribute to society.
The optimist invents the aeroplane,
the pessimist the parachute.

Consider being one of those who invents the soaring airplane, not the dropping parachute. Choose to be filled with joy every chance that you can get. Live a healthier longer life. As this chapter's quote states,

Joy in your soul is nutrition for your heart.

10

Living with Joy

Our thoughts shape our wills.

On the topics of emotional outlooks and airplanes mentioned in the previous chapter, I share this incident.

Some time ago, while waiting to board a plane, my attention was drawn to a woman sitting not far from me in the boarding lounge. She was continually issuing epic sighs and mumbling audible complaints to everyone and no one special. Her topics ranged from the waiting time for boarding to the noise in the area to needing a bigger chair to whatever else she did not appreciate. Weary passengers kept taking the vacant seat beside her. Then after a few minutes, they willingly stood up and moved away. Consciously choosing to stand and wait rather than sit beside her.

When the crew started the boarding process I admit to not being too thrilled when, muttering loudly, she moved into the line beside me. Physically she appeared to be in good health for a woman her age and size. She capably hefted an over-sized purse and a tapestry bag carry-on that bulged beyond anything I had ever seen. A strapping redcap would have buckled under its weight. Obviously she was neither weak nor infirmed.

She followed me the entire length of the jet way, naturally grousing about the long walk. She did not consider that the jet way had to be long enough to reach the entrance door of the jumbo aircraft. At the end of the jet way she kvetched because the curtains had not been tightly secured between the end of the jet way and the plane's surface. No mind that the day was lovely and the fresh air and warm sun felt delightful as I stepped from the jet way unto the plane.

Fortunately her seat was several rows ahead of mine. However, at the end of the flight, as we de-planed, there she was again. I stopped to allow her to get into the aisle. She did not have time to thank me for being courteous. Rather, she busied herself whining about the distance between her seat and the one ahead of her. It had not suited her. Given her size in comparison to most of the passengers on the plane, the complaint was real, notwithstanding the circumstances that no doubt created her complaint. They probably included copious times when she over-indulged in too many buffet lines.

I should add that the plane arrived well ahead of schedule. The flight was akin to floating in air. The landing had been seamless. None of those details seemed noteworthy events to that lady. Nothing, nothing, nothing suited her. Everything presented issues to contend with in emphatic negative fashions.

As our ways parted she left my space as she had entered it, heaving whopping sighs and loudly grumbling about everything. Life for her was one, immense, on-going crisis. It could be assumed that nothing good will happen in her life because she would not tolerate it.

The negative vibrations she dispatched that day were convulsive. She siphoned energy from anyone unfortunate enough to be near her. As a cynically unhealthy person, she seemingly thought it was the rest of the world that was unhealthy. Unlike little Pooh Bear, there would never be a perfect day, or year, or world for her.

Like Dr. Fleming, I do not consider anything in life an accident. So I wondered what good could ever come from the encounter with her. Then I realized it was a noteworthy experience, a bona fide example of pessimism in action, a concrete illustration of an unfortunate joyless lifestyle. And, it bore out a well-known statistic. Each of us has an energy field around ourselves. Energy levels are quickly picked-up by others. Therefore, 25% of our mood depends on the moods of those around us. With that thought, I immediately shed the 25% of negativity that lady had deposited with me. I moved on with the rest of my journey completely untroubled.

An example of optimism, and assuredly a more uplifting anecdote, is this next one.

I know a woman who has been active all her life. She marched as head majorette with her high school band. After graduation she took a secretarial position and in her off-hours modeled professionally. She swam and played tennis long past her 65th birthday. Over the years, she entertained many guests in her home, mothered two children, earned a college degree, and taught school for 25 years. Plus, all her life she worked tirelessly for humanitarian causes.

Her active life screeched to an abrupt halt several years ago when she fell down seven steps in her home and broke a leg in three places. The breaks required surgery and then a long period of rehabilitation to mend her leg. I remember sitting in the waiting room during her second surgery. When the doctor came out, to my relief, he announced the procedure had been successful. Seventeen screws held the metal support plate he had attached to her right tibia. The sad news came when he predicted she would probably not walk again without assistance. At best she might walk with a cane. At worst she would be wheelchair bound.

Then followed months in a care facility. The doctor scheduled physical therapy for her once a day, but she went twice a day. There can be no question her determination to resume her former active life helped boost her spirits and her healing. After a year she walked under her own power to a car waiting to take her home.

Today she lives alone. She walks unaided. She goes up and

down the same stairs where she once fell. She has resumed her active life. She sits on boards, raises funds for favorite projects, and reaps community awards for her commitments and outstanding service.

During her recuperation she certainly had "down times." Any experience that life altering and traumatic on all levels is going to send even the best of us into tailspins. Nonetheless, she finally came to grips with her mental distress. When she did, she regained a productive outlook and her emotional balance. She focused on moving forward, determined to enjoy herself and her life, just as she had done before the fall.

There you have two women. One spewed venom in her wake with every step. Yet she capably carried hand luggage that would have staggered even the most robust of porters. The other was maimed by an inopportune fall. She had to learn to walk again. However, as a staunch believer in the power of thinking positively, she worked diligently, and "stepped" forward physically, mentally, and socially.

If they ever board the same aircraft, one will carp when she notices the curtain not attached to the side of the plane. The other will smile when she feels a warm breeze brush her shoulders as she steps aboard. She would agree that it is best to,

Choose to be optimistic,
it feels better.

That bit of succinct advice comes from the 14th Dalai Lama (1935-) who is a staunch advocate of peace and joy. As a leading supporter of showering gentleness on all living things, the Dalai Lama represents a sterling example of how to live optimistically. He was designated in childhood to become a monk. In 2013, and at 78-years of age, he is the longest living incumbent to the high seat. Through his many years steeped in faith, he grew into maturity always aware that the heart and soul are best nourished by joy, *"it feels better."*

On the topic of optimism and joy, in his autobiography *Long Walk to Freedom* Nelson Mandela (1918-) wrote the following,

I am fundamentally an optimist.
Whether that comes from nature or nurture,
I cannot say.
Part of being optimistic is
keeping one's head pointed toward the sun,
one's feet moving forward.
There were many dark moments
when my faith in humanity was sorely tested,
but I would not and could not
give myself up to despair.
That way lays defeat and death.

A firm believer in positive thinking, Mandela knew the sunlit highs and the moonless lows in his lifetime. On numerous occasions he refused to *"give myself up to despair."* He saw in others' lives *"that way lays defeat and death."*

Accused of inciting union strikes and leaving South Africa without permission, he spent 27 years in prison beginning in 1964. After his release, he assumed an active political role as a champion for human rights and anti-apartheid. Between 1994 and 1999, he served as South Africa's first black president. He was inaugurated at the age of 77. A survivor of tuberculosis and prostate cancer, as well as having suffered severe physical abuse during his years of incarceration, he doggedly refused to allow the weight of negativity to seep into his soul. If ever an individual understood the power of optimism and living with joy, that man would be Nelson Mandela.

As Mandela knew, what you hold in your amazing mind affects your overall well being. It affects the way you appear to others, your countenance. In James 1:23 that point is succinctly summed up with,

Man looks at the outward appearance,
but the Lord looks at the heart.

While the Lord looks at what is inside, the whole person mirrors the thoughts of the mind. Mandela did not hold in his mind what he did not want in his life. Instead he worked for the positivity of change. Undeniably, our physical lives and our souls are acutely affected by what we hold in our minds. In *The Old Testament's* Book of Proverbs 23:7, part of the verse reads,

...For as he thinketh in his heart,
so is he.

That verse became the inspiration for a self-help book written by James Allen (1864-1912). Allen was an early, 20th Century, front-runner in the field of self-help and motivational advocacy publications. Published in 1902, *As a Man Thinketh* was his third book. So timeless was its message, the book is still in mass production. Allen opened his book with this poem:

Mind is the Master power that molds and makes,
And Man is Mind, and evermore he takes
The tool of Thought, and, shaping what he wills,
Brings forth a thousand joys, a thousand ills:
He thinks in secret, and it comes to pass:
Environment is but his looking glass.

The phrase *"He thinks in secret, and it comes to pass"* is akin to the phrase "the power of intention." The internationally recognized lecturer Wayne Dyer is a respected authority in the field of self-improvement and spirituality. In Dyer's book *The Power of Intention* he shares his thoughts on the subject. Dyer says,

Intention is a field of energy
that flows invisibly beyond the reach
of our normal, everyday habitual patterns…

(It is the indescribable) powerful energy a person feels when inspired.
…meaning "in spirit."

Dyer sees intention as a positive force in the Universe. He says it is a force continually accessible to us, but not always accessed by us. Instead of struggling to reach goals by sheer will and might, Dyer suggests that we tap into the power of intention that rests within each of us as,

a spiritual orientation where healing,
creating miracles,
manifesting, and making a connection
to divine intelligence are genuine possibilities.

…anything we can conceive on in our minds…
while staying in harmony with
the universal all-creating Source…
can and must come to pass.

Hence, lucky people are more than "just lucky;" they habitually access their powers of intention. Living with the positivity of intention makes it possible to drive down the road of life, according to Dyer, with,

...an endless stream of green lights before you!

Dyer makes a convincing case for living with hope and joy and optimistic thinking. The one caution is to stay *"in harmony with the universal all-creating Source."* To quote Allen, again,

Right thinking begins
with the words we say to ourselves.

"...the words we say to ourselves" are power-filled. Our thoughts shape our wills. They can *"bring(s) forth a thousand joys,"* or *"a thousand ills."* Our thoughts make us what we are and who we are. Our minds are mega-influencers. Our thoughts have the power to intentionally bring good or bad into our lifetimes on Spaceship Earth.

You are in charge. Therefore, you cannot help but bring your thoughts to your own reality and parade them before the public. You have probably heard the popular adage,

Your face is your own fault after 40.

There is truth in that quip. By 40, what is inside of you has crept out and makes itself known on the outside of you. The lines on your face, the set of your jaw, the deep furrows (or not) on your brow, the slump or slope or squaring of your shoulders, the stresses and/or delights you internalized will all begin to make themselves known to the world. The optimistic joys and/or the pessimistic patterns of your thoughts etch themselves on your face and reflect in your total countenance. What a splendid and wholesome goal it should be to continually strive to be the "image of joy."

Our miraculous mind, that shapeless, space-less form within us, is a forceful participant in the quality of our time on Spaceship Earth. Purposefully thinking joy filled thoughts will not automatically guarantee longevity or a pile of money, but it surely assists in bringing quality to our lives and richness to our days.

Like love, joy intentionally arrived on Earth with you. Joy is an integral part of your eternal soul, a connector to your Source. As the extraordinary miracle that you are, when you choose… choose joy.

11

Enjoying Your Joy

Enjoying joy and causing joy is the best of both worlds.

WE ARE ABLE TO CARRY five thoughts in our minds at a time. Four are on the subconscious level and one consciously. By divine design, the mind only allows us to feel one emotion and think one thought at a time. So, we can be upbeat or beaten up. But we cannot be beaten up and upbeat at the same time.

Here is an example on that point.

Imagine that you are depressed, angry, impatient, or perhaps just agitated. Suddenly the phone rings. The party on the other end of the ringing phone has no idea of your mental and emotional states. Since your discontent is not their fault, when you begin to speak with them you are forced to "shift gears." You have to stop muttering and gritting your teeth. For the length of time you speak with the other party, you ignore your perturbed state. Circumstances demand that you speak politely and calmly. You relax and enjoy a cordial chat.

When the call ends you hang up the receiver. Mentally and emotionally you are no longer the person who picked up the receiver of the ringing phone. In fact, you might not straightaway recall what it was that caused you to be so irritable. Your mind (and the calling party) came to your rescue. Now you are in a "different place." After the phone conversation you feel just fine.

The point here is that holding two opposing emotions in your conscious mind at one time is not possible. Of the two, positive energy is the dominant force. In any competition, optimism will always win. It overpowers pessimism. Optimism carries within itself high levels of energy vibrations. Positive energy empowers and overwhelms weaker forces. It pushes away negative forces.

As explored in the previous chapter, optimism and pessimism are states of mind. They strongly influence your perspectives on living. They affect your health and interactions with society. They color your outlooks on life. On that point, the Roman Emperor Marcus Aurelius made this appropriate entry in his diary,

The soul becomes dyed
with the color of its thoughts.

It is fascinating the Aurelius chose to use color as a metaphor for your thoughts and your soul.

Colors are actually vibrations of light and they play significant roles in your daily life. How they are integrated into environments affects how you react. Perhaps you are aware that the color orange is a popular restaurant hue because it stimulates the appetite. If orange and turquoise are used together in a dining facility decor, statistics show people eat more food. Hospitals regularly use soft greens, blues, and peach colors because they actually quicken patients' recovery periods. The color blue calms and lowers the respiration and the blood pressure, while red does just the reverse. Imagine your emotional state if a dentist is standing over you, hovering with a loud whirling drill in his hand, while you are reclined in a procedure room chair staring at a ceiling painted crimson red.

On some level we all understand the impact colors have on our moods or why else would we say, "red hot," "green with envy," "under a black cloud," "in a blue mood," "tickled pink"...? Colors cannot be under estimated, they are powerful influences on us socially, psychologically, and symbolically.

If you opened a box of 150 crayons, what colors would you

pick from the box to represent the souls of the two women I introduced to you in Chapter 10? Surely the color your choose to symbolize the bemoaning airline traveler would not be the same color you would decide on to represent the upbeat community leader. Today what color would you select from the box of crayons to represent yourself?

As there are many colors affecting your life, undeniably you are also born with inclinations toward specific personality traits and physical conditions. However, other influences affect you as well.

1. Your environment plays a major role in how you manage your time.
2. Your experiences impact heavily on your viewpoints.
3. However, how you choose to look at life has the most significant influence.

If all the above influences were in the audience for a dramatic production of your life, where would the ushers seat them? "Experiences" and "environment," which you can, more often than not exercise some control over, would be seated in the balcony. While "how you choose to look at life" would be in the front row, center seat. Critical to the quality of your time on Earth is how you view and value life.

You arrived with a pre-ordained destiny. You brought your lesson plans, your purposes with you. You know on the highest level of your super consciousness your reasons for being on this planet at this very moment. You are in charge of you. You are the star and the director. The success or failure of the show rests on your shoulders. No blame games in this production. Your goal is a sustained standing ovation after the final curtain call.

As I touched on earlier, fixed characteristics came with us to Earth. Other circumstances we confront here and we either nurture them or overcome them. Regardless of experiences and environment, ultimately we choose the emotional window through which we want to see our world, to look at life. The window can be smog-covered and colorless, or clear and bright. The dusty dinginess of one window will block the sun, while another right beside it radiates with the spectrum of a rainbow. Dark heavy drapes hang at one opening, while another stands curtain-free, flung open to let in the world. The famous, often funny, Irish, playwright and literary critic, George Bernard Shaw once quipped,

Better keep yourself clean and bright;
you are the window
through which you must see the world.

Shaw's advice is worth repeating, *"You are the window through which you must see the world."*

Add to that the popular idiom,

"Your eyes are the windows to your soul."

Your transparent eyes are unmistakably revealing. They display to the world the honesty, the deceit, the hunger, the fear, the love, the sadness, the delights of your mind and your soul. When a seriously ill person nears the last days of their time on Earth, often their eyes become crystalline. They swim with the glistening presence of their soul. Their soul is preparing to go home. If you look directly into your own eyes, you will see that your eyes reflect your mind's thoughts and thus your soul.

In the meantime, as you move through your days, how you

see what you see is vitally important. Nearly everything can be looked at from more than one perspective: cute or disgusting, gloomy or glorious, lovable or despicable, glamorous or gaudy. Each person decides. Just remember,

Optimism will liven you up.
Pessimism will wipe you out.
The decision is yours.

During his years on Earth, Jesus "practiced what he preached." In spite of all the disruptions and disruptive encounters, he determined how he wanted to look at life. Much is assumed, but too little is made of Jesus' cheerfulness and his happiness when *The New Testament* is studied. Nevertheless, Jesus absolutely radiated with excitement, vitality, love, and joy. He lived a life filled with adventure. He smiled, he laughed, and he talked with his companions. He climbed the sunlit hills of Judea. He walked the breeze swept shores of the Sea of Galilee. He looked down into the bright smiling faces of children and up at the twinkling stars in the vast darkness of night. He genuinely enjoyed being human and joy filled. Jesus lived, as he believed. Like it or not, you live as you believe, too.

Of course, Marcus Aurelius had something to say about all of this. His comment being,

Dwell on the beauty of life.
Watch the stars,
and see yourself running with them.

"Dwell on the beauty of life" and run with the stars. What a spectacularly beautiful image that evokes.

When I want to go to a serene place in my mind, one that is

perfect for me to *"dwell on,"* I am 6-years old. And I am running through a meadow lush with tall grasses warmed by the gentle heat of the day; I can smell the moistness of the earth. I pass bright daisies and little yellow cowslips and buttercups. I hear the contented droning of honeybees as they buzz from one plump blossom of clover to another. I notice the lazy floating butterflies. The sun shines down from a blue cloudless sky. My hair waves behind me; I am released and happy. I am in a tranquil and wonderful place. What joy and abandon that vision brings to my mind.

Perhaps you have such a place where you go to *"dwell on the beauty of life."* Maybe your vision takes you on a relaxing stroll along a wide, pebble-strewn beach. The late afternoon sun softly toasts your back, while gentle waves quietly break and splash around your ankles. Overhead a trio of gulls swoops and floats on the drafts of the cool ocean breezes, and your peaceful thoughts float with them. Or, it could be that your vision takes you to a quiet shady respite in a park, or maybe you, too, run with the stars as you *"dwell on the beauty of life."*

Interesting how we tend to seek to be close to the nurturing powers of nature in quiet times. In any account, having a place to go to in your thoughts where you are free and safe and happy is a healthy habit. It allows you to travel within yourself. It draws joy and peace into your being.

On the topic of drawing joy into your being, here is an account of a man who undeniably survived by drawing joy into himself.

Lew was a robust, athletic, self-made man. Well into his 60's, it shocked him to learn he had cancer. By the time the doctors discovered the disease, it had moved into a late stage. Lew took quick action. He immediately checked into the Sloan-Kettering

Cancer Center in New York City. He insisted on a private room because Lew had a plan. It involved renting a truckload of situation comedy re-runs.

During his extended hospitalization, he refused to watch any news broadcasts, read any newspapers or magazines, or tolerate any tales of woe from well-meaning friends and relatives. Their visits to see him had to be positive and upbeat or they were not welcome. There would be no bad vibrations, no gloom, no sad eyes, no "what if's" or "if only's," and no pity parties in Lew's room.

Along with "Lew's Laws" for hospital visits, he dutifully followed the prescribed medical treatments and endured the necessary surgeries. The rest of the time he watched comedy shows. And that was what all his visitors did as well. He laughed. They laughed. Everyone laughed.

The shows he chose were the genre of the 1950-60's *Red Skeleton Show* with the knockabout red-haired comedian's goofy impersonations of made-up characters like Clem Kadiddlehopper and Willie Lump-Lump. His skits of "Gertrude and Heathcliff, the Two Seagulls" always drew huge waves of laughter. Skeleton imitated them by lisping, crossing his eyes, and sticking his thumbs into his armpits so he could flap his elbows for "wings."

Another favorite series was *The Carol Barnett Show.* Along with the top-notch comedienne, Barnett, were free wheeling comics like Vickie Lawrence, Harvey Korman, and Tim Conway. The entire cast's unscripted impromptu capers, that left even them bewildered and hysterical, guaranteed sustained howls of laughter.

The *Mary Tyler Moore Show,* with Ed Asner as Lou Grant, Mary's tough acting, tenderhearted boss, brought refreshing lines and kooky tangled situations. The entire crew was a rollicking troop. It included Betty White, who played the sniveling, little, conniving home economist, Sue Ann Nivens. On the show "man-hungry" Sue Ann unabashedly chased after skitterish Lou Grant when she was not on the uproariously hilarious and catastrophic stage set of her "The Happy Homemaker" show.

You get the drift. As the weeks and months tumbled by, Lew slowly began to recover. The doctors expressed their relief that the cancer treatments seemed to be working. But, what worked even more than their medical efforts was that Lew chose to be happy and laugh. And, in the process, he never dwelled on negative world or personal news, other people's troubles, his own fragile fate, or concern himself for one minute with "how he felt."

In time, Lew walked out of his hospital room and back into his very active public life. His doctors believed their efforts contributed to his healing, but agreed Lew literally laughed himself healthy. Sometime later Lew passed on, but his personal efforts to extend his life gave him many more years and many more opportunities to laugh. Lew had added opportunities to be filled with joy. Happiness is healthy. With Lew as an example, it seems laughter really is the best medicine, or at least a sensible prescription to add to all medical treatment procedures.

Joy is an entirely positive emotion. With joy's laughter comes affirming energy that permeates every part of the body. Affirming energy vibrates the space around you as well as floods the space inside you. Laughter, as a close relative of joy, really does heal your mind and body and nourish your soul. Laughter truly does "warm your heart."

As mentioned earlier, the mind is an amazing member of our miraculous being and the site of an intensely active arena. The average person processes about 60,000 thoughts a day while using only about 10% of their mental capacity. That's all… 10%. How frightening to consider that if your mind is flooded with negative thoughts that 10% commands enough sway to destroy your body, the quality of your days, and your life itself. Likewise, if 10% of your mind is full of positive thoughts, that 10% of is enough to heal your body and mind and enrich your soul. We each decide how it will be. Clearly the potential for success, satisfaction, and good health rests within us much more than we realize.

One of America's early colonists and an esteemed Founding Father was Benjamin Franklin (1706-1790). In conversation he once noted,

The Constitution only guarantees the American people
the right to pursue happiness.
You have to catch it for yourself.

And, considered to be a specialist on positive thinking, the Dalai Lama once remarked,

Happiness is not something ready made.
It comes from your own actions.

Both the Dalai Lama and Franklin spoke truths. You must pursue your own happiness. You must *"catch it for yourself."* No one else can assume the burden of being responsible for giving your life meaning. *"It comes from your own actions."* It is your job. The mission belongs to you. You are exactly what you allow inside yourself. Your thoughts are powerful, even if you only use 10% of your potential.

Just as researchers found that optimists live longer and have more rewarding lives, their studies also demonstrated that when positive efforts and habits are intentionally put into action they can and will vibrate around the world. When a good deed or kindness is shown, it generates feelings in others that are positive and affirming. It sends ripples of affirming waves out into the Universe. By its nature, meaning the energy of its vibrations, good travels at high rates of speed and for long periods of time.

But, then it did not take an army of mental health specialists to tell my dear Mother that. For as long as I can remember, whenever anyone thanked my Mother for an act of goodwill she had extended, her customary response was to say, "Thank you. Now, just pass it on."

That is a splendid response to make to any good deed or genuine compliment or gracious gesture. "Just pass it on" to the next person. Doing that will generate positive vibrations in others and the good travels and travels and travels some more.

As an example:

If you are sitting at an On Ramp and another motorist slows to let you move into the traffic flow, you are more likely to return the favor by slowing and/or motioning to another driver waiting at the next On Ramp. In this case good really does travel, literally and figuratively. We pass it on and on and on.

And while on the subjects of joy and travelling, according to a 2012 study, the country of Denmark holds the title of the happiest place to live. Denmark qualifies in the areas of material living conditions, quality of life, environment, governance, health, life satisfaction, safety, and work-to leisure balance. If you would like a few options, consider any of the Scandinavian countries. They all made the top 10 list. Switzerland, Iceland, Holland, Austria, and Canada rank high as well. Depending on the survey (and several are conducted every few years) the USA ranks as number 11. Out of the 155 countries included in one study, the number 11 slot is just fine with me. As an American, I am happy to accept that survey's evaluation.

No matter where we live in this world, none of us realize

everything we want in life, but we always get what we expect. We get what we intend that we will get. Like powerful magnets, our thoughts attract to us what we hold in our minds. Since positive energy easily overpowers negative energy, deliberately focusing on the good and the joy filled makes life so much more rewarding. When in doubt, pick the power of optimism.

In summation, your lifetime is precious. You did not arrive on Spaceship Earth with a plan to purposely waste your years. What would be the sense in that effort? You are important to yourself, your world, and your God. Keep the healthiness of joy in your heart. Take a page out of Milne's book and be akin to perky little Pooh Bear. Make every day your favorite day and as special as it is.

Let your soul be one of the bright crayons in the box. Run with the stars. Know the world is enriched with every joy you enjoy, all the laughter you share, and the many happinesses you bring into the lives of others.

Joy, like love, is a central part of your emotional and spiritual make up. It is designed to offer your journey richness and fullness. It encourages you to be truly and totally human. Joy allows you to live in harmony with yourself, with others in your world, and with your God. Enjoy your joy.

12
Be What You Believe

Intend to be all you believe you can be.

OVER 120 YEARS AGO, MY Great Aunt Hazel was born in 1891. She grew up in the little town of Stoneboro in rural northwestern Pennsylvania. She was the younger of my Grandfather's two sisters. According to family lore she must have been a bit of a spitfire, especially for a young woman growing up at the end of the prim and proper, china teacup, white lace gloved Victorian Era. She thoroughly enjoyed times filled with lots of laughter, all types of dancing, pretty clothes, handsome men, and being married. Sometimes she must have exasperated my Great Grandparents, but everyone agreed that Hazel Doyle was a beautiful vivacious woman who unreservedly loved life.

Marriage in the early 1900's was a forever contract. No matter what adverse personal matters couples dealt with behind closed doors, they stayed married. That having been said, Hazel married four times. The first marriage did not last long because she and Allen eloped. Her longsuffering parents did not take well to that surprise. Nor did they consider it proper for their daughter to begin marriage by escaping out an upstairs window and climbing down a ladder in the middle of the night. So, they took the proper steps and had the marriage annulled. Later, Hazel admitted,

I suppose I really didn't love Allen all that much.
But it sure was an adventure at the time.

Not too long after the annulment Hazel married again. But she divorced her second husband. When they "courted" she did not realize Bill was such a heavy imbiber. When his drinking habits turned disruptive to their home life, and because they had a small daughter, Hazel filed for a divorce. Social pressures or not, she did not want their daughter, Ruth, to be raised in that sort of unpredictable environment.

The last two men Hazel married were handsome wonderful charmers. First came Great Uncle Fred. As a successful businessman, Fred owned a lovely restaurant. It was a popular destination that attracted diners seeking artfully presented delicious food served in a gracious setting. She willingly worked with him at the business, and they provided well for themselves. After Fred died, Hazel married Great Uncle Andy. A number of years her junior, he, too, was a fine addition to the family. However, Hazel out-lived him as well.

Throughout her long and engaging life, Great Aunt Hazel had a host of practices to which she religiously adhered. Most of them had to do with how she disciplined herself. There were ones like:

» Always keep your shoulders back.

» When you get up out of a chair, walk like you are going some place.

» Never leave the bedroom in the morning until you have combed your hair and put on some make-up.

Hazel had her standards. She was a gracious person and a 24/7 glamorous gal her entire life.

One of Great Aunt Hazel's practices was somewhat novel. She positively believed that if she wore red shoes she would have fun. Even into her 70's, a shoebox with a pair of red shoes in it sat on the back seat of her longer-than-a-city-block, chrome encrusted, 1950's Buick Riviera. She kept the shoes on hand in case she decided she wanted to have a good time, or if a good time suddenly came along that she did not want to miss. Magically, when she wore her red shoes, Great Aunt Hazel literally "took over the room" and had the best time of anyone in it.

Perhaps because she believed in the power of her red shoes, or because my memories of her are so fond (Even though she barked at me for slumping my shoulders.), I always keep a pair of red shoes on hand. If they worked for Great Aunt Hazel, how could they not work for me! Influence is influence. Believing is believing. Even when it is believing in the power of a pair of red shoes!

Now, let me share a story about another person who believed, but almost did not *need* shoes. His name was Glenn.

Glenn and his older brother used to get up early on wintry Kansas mornings and trudge to the one-room school they attended. On those mornings their job was to get the school warm before classes commenced. They enjoyed starting the day's fire in the black, iron, pot-bellied stove. Unfortunately, one morning there was a terrible explosion. Someone had mistakenly switched the kerosene they used to ignite the fire for gasoline. The ensuing inferno badly damaged the schoolhouse. Tragically, Glenn's 13-year old brother died in the blaze. Luckily, someone was able to drag 8-year old Glenn out of the flames. However, he suffered critical injuries.

The entire lower half of Glenn's body was devastated. He had lost all the toes on his left foot. Most of the nerves and the tissues along his legs and around his knees were completely gone. The doctors told his parents he would not survive. When Glenn did survive, the doctors wanted to amputate his legs. They predicted they were useless, that he would never walk again. Little Glenn overheard what the doctors told his family. Fortunately he became so distraught about not having any legs, that his parents rejected the amputation idea. Opting to just be thankful to *have* him. Sadly realizing he would be wheelchair bound the rest of his life.

At home, after his protracted hospital stay, his parents spent hours rubbing his lifeless legs trying to bring feeling back into them. Their efforts yielded little change. But even at his young age, Glenn believed he would walk again. He determined that somehow he would. He did not know how, but he would. When the Kansas weather turned pleasant the following spring, his mother wheeled him out into the back yard to get some sun every afternoon.

Now, fast-forward to two years after the accident. The year is 1919. One day while he sat in the back yard getting his daily dose of fresh air and sunshine, Glenn intentionally slipped from the wheel chair. Then the 10-year old pulled himself across the yard, his frail legs dragging behind him. His target was the picket fence that rimmed their property. Once at the fence, Glenn reached up and grasped the top of the pickets. He struggled to pull himself up. His goal was to try to stand. Each day he did that. Gradually his legs became stronger, until at last he could stand. Then he began moving along the fence. Haltingly he drew one leg in front of the other, walking as best he could. He did that day-after-day-after-day. Eventually he wore a smooth dirt track along the picket fence. With time he found he could walk alone, and finally he began to run.

When Glenn was at long last able to return to school, he ran. He ran to school every day. He ran everywhere. In high school he ran on his track team. He participated in that sport during his college years as well. The sheer joy of having his legs, of being able to use his legs, and to run was exhilarating for him.

Now, fast-forward again. During the Summer Olympics of 1932 and 1936, Glenn Cunningham (1909-1988) successfully represented America as a distance runner. Between those four years, Glenn continued to train and enter races. On June 16, 1934, in Madison Square Garden in New York City, Cunningham stepped up to the starting line of a mile race. He waited for the signal and when it went off he began to run. And, he ran faster than anyone had ever run. He ran the mile in 4:06.8 minutes and broke the world's record. All his track accomplishments are impressive on their own; but knowing the story behind his successes makes them even more unprecedented.

During World War II, Cunningham spent two years in the Navy. He is credited with establishing new physical training programs at both The Great Lakes and the San Diego bases. Later, Dr. Glenn Cunningham founded a youth camp in Kansas for troubled children. The estimate is that well over 10,000 children with difficulties benefited from their times at his camp. He and his wife managed the camp until his death in 1988.

Glenn Cunningham believed. From the day of his terrible accident he believed first that he would live; then he believed that he would live and not be crippled. Despite all the odds, he believed that he would walk. He was a single-minded child and a man of great faith. Through all the time of his healing his favorite Bible verse was Isaiah 40:31,

But those who wait on the Lord
shall renew their strength;
they shall mount up with wings like eagles,
they shall run and not be weary,
they shall walk and not faint.

He both walked and ran. He was not weary and he did not faint. Glenn Cunningham's life is about setting goals and believing. Through engaging in single-minded determination, ambition, courage, and faith, he intentionally achieved his aspirations. He brought to his body what he thought in his mind.

Glenn Cunningham serves as a commanding example of what an individual is capable of accomplishing. He changed his world, and eventually the worlds of countless children, by what he believed he could do.

His doctors had deemed what he achieved to be impossible. But he did it. Like miracles, nothing is impossible, maybe improbable, but not impossible. We change our world by what we determine to do. If we believe in miracles, they will happen. The one constant ingredient, which must be there from the start-to-the-finish, is believing.

In order to succeed,
we must first believe that we can.

The prolific, 20th Century, Greek writer Nikos Kazantzakis (1883-1957) originated that quote. More a philosopher than an author, his works include two that became movies: *Zorba the Greek* and *The Last Temptation of Christ.* Kazantzakis' strong beliefs and his insights into life with all its glories and mysteries continue to be an unending intellectual adventure for both scholars and critics.

Life is a series of decisions. Some decisions are big, some are small, some are non-consequential. Some can be life threatening and others life enhancing. Every situation presents choices, but *"In order to succeed, we must first believe that we can."* We can choose to believe and be optimistic, which leads to success, or we can choose to be pessimistic, which leads to staying stuck. It is your life. It is your choice. You decide what you want to believe.

Here is a recount of a remarkable woman. Like Glenn Cunningham, she had dreams and a firm belief that her dreams would come true.

Betsy's young life appeared grim when at 2-years of age she

contracted polio. Her frantic parents insisted the best doctors see her. They were always hopeful that some how the disease would not leave her severely handicapped for life. But, it did.

Long before wide doors on public buildings automatically swung open and handicapped ramps made crossing intersections easier, Betsy made the decision that she wanted to physically attend high school. She intended to be like the other students, even if she was wheelchair bound. She not only attended the local public school, but she never missed a day. She graduated with honors.

At 17-years of age, Betsy had an additional aspiration. She wanted to be a teacher, so during her senior year in high school she applied to area colleges. She did not indicate on the application form that she was handicapped. When the college of her choice accepted her, she showed up on campus in her wheelchair. The admissions department officials were aghast. They tried to gently explain to her that she would never be able to handle the course load. They kindly suggested she try one or two classes the first semester to see if college really was for her. Determined and believing in her abilities, Betsy made the officials a counter-offer. If they would approve her carrying a full load of classes for one semester, and if she passed all her exams, they would stop concerning themselves with her academic future. At the close of the first semester they stopped worrying.

Betsy graduated on time and quickly found a high school teaching position. In a hand-control, equipped car, she drove herself to work every day. She wheeled herself into the building, and made the trip to her classroom unaided. She also accepted the cheerleading advisor and girls tennis coach positions.

Still, Betsy's dreams had not been entirely fulfilled. She wanted a family of her own. Eventually she learned she could privately adopt an infant boy. But, she had to prove to the agency she could care for him herself. Betsy, also, had to prove she could capably maintain her lifestyle and financially support the child. So, she continued to teach school, coach the tennis team, and advise the cheerleaders, all the while caring for her infant child. She did it all.

In order for the adoption to be finalized she needed a van specifically equipped to take her new son with her and easily get him in and out of the vehicle. On the West Coast she located a man named Ted. He equipped vans for handicapped people. Betsy called him. He agreed to purchase the van she wanted, equip it to her specifications, drive it across country, and teach her how to use it. He did just that.

As it turned out, Ted knew a lot about equipping handicapped vehicles. At the age of 12 his legs had been crushed between two cars. He, too, was handicapped. You guessed it. Ted and Betsy eventually married, and Ted adopted her son. To mark the second year of their marriage, they took "their son" with them on an anniversary trip.

Like Glenn Cunningham, Betsy believed she could realize her goals. So she did. She refused to let pessimistic thoughts or the negative attitudes of others sway her from her dreams. Betsy drew to herself that which she believed the Universe could bring to her. With determination, ambition, courage, and faith, Betsy managed to live her life her way. And, the Source of all power gladly assisted her with her intentions.

Multitudes of us are blessed with the abilities to walk and talk and see and hear. Yet, we sometimes look at the troubles in our lives as insurmountable obstacles. In those times we would do well to consider what real obstacles others have confronted and beaten. Although they faced demanding mountains, Glenn

Cunningham and Betsy both made it to the top. They were born as "regular people," but they are outstanding examples of success. You must know of others.

Managing your life is your responsibility. Environmental circumstances, family conditions, educational backgrounds, financial issues, physical handicaps, race, gender, religion… . There can be no excuses. You are the only one that puts limits on your personal will. Believe that your miraculous life is yours for the making and it will be.

And, no one is ever "too old" or "too young." If you are alive you are accountable. It does nothing for you, or the world around you, if you warily creep along making lame excuses, just getting by, or endlessly waiting for someone to do for you what you should be doing for yourself. Take a page out of the books of my friend Betsy or Glenn Cunningham or use my Great Aunt Hazel's book (well, maybe not the number of marriages part), but certainly the positive outlook part. Believe that you can make your life a memorable adventure and it will be as you intend and perhaps even more.

Inside of us are immeasurable energies and forces. We are all part of one, great, vibrating Universe, one Whole, one Source. We are all so much more capable than we often allow ourselves to be. Determine to be, intend to be, and then become all that you believe.

The next chapter relates another true story about a family of resilient believers. Individuals who let nothing, not even death and disablement, keep them from realizing their dream. And one of our great cities is the beneficiary of their optimistic determination.

13

Believe in Your Dreams

The solution to a problem starts when you believe you can solve it.

In the late 1860's, the German-born American, civil engineer, John Roebling (1806-1869) dreamed of connecting Brooklyn to Manhattan Island with a bridge. At the time, national and international bridge experts said it could not be done. One after another told him to forget the "hair-brained idea." Their arguments included the excessive distance from shore to shore, and the fact the bridge would have to span a wide body of deep, fast running water. On the Brooklyn side of the East River the depth is 44.5-feet, but on the Manhattan side the depth drops to 78.5-feet.

Obsessed with his dream, Roebling would not be dissuaded. He believed that to ease transportation routing in and out of New York City, a bridge had to be built in lower Manhattan. Eventually he convinced his son, Washington (1837-1926), who was 32-years old at the time and also a civil engineer, to help him draw-up the preliminary plans. The elder Roebling just knew that by using wire cables the feat could be achieved.

John Roebling had patented wire cabling in 1842. The inspiration for his idea came from working on the Erie Canal's digging sites north of Pittsburgh. At that time, using inclined planes, men dragged barges from the railway off-loading stops to the canal with 9-inch diameter hemp ropes. One time a rope snapped and killed a worker. That accident deeply disturbed Roebling. Like hemp rope, the steel, wire rope cables he invented were designed to be flexible. But they would not break and could manage considerable weight.

At last, in early 1869, he received the "go ahead" to build his

1595.5-foot bridge over the East River. After significant detailed planning, the project seemed to be off to an impressive start. However, a few months into it a dreadful accident occurred at the site. A ferryboat crashed into the dock where John Roebling was standing while he took measurements for the Brooklyn tower. His leg was crushed. All the toes on his right foot had to be amputated. Then lockjaw set in. Through his deep wounds, he contracted tetanus. Unfortunately, two weeks after the accident he died on July 22, 1869.

Tragedy continued to stalk the project and the family. Included in the accidents were a fire, an explosion, a contract dispute, and men suffering (and some even dying) from "the bends." The bends was a condition caused from working in the deep water below the East River to set the caissons that would eventually support the bridge. Moving too suddenly from high-pressure to low-pressure environments caused the medical condition. Today's deep-sea divers must use caution when diving or surfacing for the same reason.

Washington Roebling was seriously hurt in an accident at the bridge site three years after the death of his father. While he was helping to extinguish a fire in one of the underwater caissons Washington got the bends. Although he survived, the episode left him unable to easily move or talk again. But, his mind had not been affected, he could think. By using one finger, he designed a way to tap on his wife Emily's arm the messages he wanted his team of construction workers to follow. Each day Emily delivered the messages. And from his apartment window on the Brooklyn side of the East River Roebling watched the construction through a telescope. About that effort, one historian commented,

Nowhere in the history of great undertakings
is there anything comparable to

(Washington) Roebling conducting the largest and most difficult engineering project ever "in absentia."

For 10 years Washington tapped out instructions with his finger on his wife's arm until the bridge was finally completed on May 24, 1883. On that day, President Grover Cleveland and Vice President Chester Arthur ceremoniously opened the longest suspension bridge in the world. Washington Roebling watched from his apartment window, as his wife Emily became the first person to walk across "their" bridge. Many citizens of New York joined in behind her to make a celebratory parade. The Brooklyn Bridge immediately became the 8th Wonder of the World.

Today the iconic and spectacular Brooklyn Bridge still stands as a tribute to the triumph of two men and one woman. It demonstrates the gritty spirit of mankind. The bridge serves as an iconic landmark for the City of New York. It boldly illustrates what strong-willed determination and believing in your dreams can do.

Immediately following the aftermath of the World Trade Center attack on September 11, 2010, the Brooklyn Bridge again played a significant role in the history of New York City. It became the main escape route for thousands fleeing lower Manhattan on foot.

If you believe, then your dream is within your grasp. There is always a path to your goal no matter what it is. The Roeblings foresaw New York City's future and wanted to build a bridge. They were told it could not be done. In spite of disasters and deaths, they carried on. They believed in their dream and refused to stop until their dream became a reality.

Dreams, inspirations, and imaginings come to us in both our sleeping and our waking hours. Like miracles, they visit us and realize themselves on their own time schedules. And we all receive different types of imaginings. Confusing, "almost real" dreams come to us in our sleep at night. Often they connect fantasy and reality in vignettes where time is inconsequential. Gentle daydreaming inspirations visit us when we are awake. And then there are those imaginings that strike us with greater force and persistence. They propel our minds into deeper thoughts, study, and often into action.

Inspirational dreams or imaginings give birth to the discoveries and inventions destined to touch all fields of mankind's endeavors and interests. Everything created by mankind was first a dream in his or her mind. The imaginations of the remarkable individuals discussed earlier in this book serve as examples of how minds powered by belief in their dreams advanced our world. The dreamers of those dreams followed the Pathways before them, and consequently they fulfilled the plans of the Universe.

No discussion on believing in dreams can go without mention of an American named Edgar Cayce (1877-1945). Often called "The Sleeping Poet," Edgar Cayce vowed as a young, Kentucky, farm boy to read the Bible every day. He kept that vow until his death in 1945. An avid churchgoer and Sunday school teacher, he is probably best remembered for his psychic readings done during self-imposed trances over a period of 43 years. Surely using more than 10% of his mental capabilities, he tapped into information beyond the limits of Earth's time and space's confines. Controversial as Cayce's activities were, his responses to clients' questions while he was in sleeplike trances were stunningly on target. For Cayce, the details he uncovered in dreams provided information about living. He once offered,

Dreams are today's answers
to tomorrow's questions.

All the dreams of Edison, Einstein, Marconi, Fleming, Fuller, Curie, Roebling, and others became the *"answers to tomorrow's questions."* If any of those individuals could be asked, they would concur with the observation by Edgar Cayce. Their inspirations visited them in timely fashions. They believed in their dreams. And their dreams became answers to our questions. Believing in our inspirations, dreams, and imaginings and acting on them is part of our journey. It is part of our Earth bound life's experiences.

One of the men who served as President of the United States during Cayce's lifetime was Calvin Coolidge (1872-1933). Nicknamed "Silent Cal," he is remembered as the President most famous for hating small talk and for speaking so seldom. Yet he became the first President to use the radio to make a public address to the American people. Coolidge served as our 29th Vice President under Warren Harding until Harding's death in 1923, when he became our 30th President for 7 years.

In contrast to his distain for small talk, Coolidge was very visible to his public. During his lifetime, he held the dubious title of being one of "the most photographed persons on earth." Coolidge never saw a camera he did not like. Although historians hold mixed reviews on his contributions to our nation, without question Coolidge is remembered as a man who believed in his dreams. He set goals and decisively saw them through to the end. In his writings was this opinion,

Nothing in the world can take
the place of persistence.
Talent will not;

nothing is more common than
unsuccessful men with talent.
Genius will not;
unrewarded genius is almost a proverb.
Education alone will not;
the world is full of educated derelicts.
Persistence and determination alone are omnipotent.
The slogan "press on" has solved
and
always will solve
the problems of the human race.

"Press on." Believe. Be determined. *"Press on."*

In 1959, Professor David J. Schwartz (1927-1987) wrote a best-selling, self-help book called *The Magic of Thinking Big.* In it he emphasized "pressing on." In his book he refers to the power of believing in yourself. Schwartz contended your dreams influence the level of what you achieve in your lifetime. One of his quotes reads,

Believe it can be done.
When you believe something can be done,
really believe,
your mind will find the ways to do it.
Believing a solution paves the way to solution.

As a former art educator I strongly support Dr. Schwartz's theory, *"Believe it can be done."* My high school art classes predictably included a composite of the entire high school, literally from one class period to the next. Some students wanted to seriously study art, to pursue it as their career path. Some students thought it would be fun to just doodle around for an hour a day and take a class where there would be no tests. Others were forced into my class. They were there as the result of a frazzled guidance counselor's last-ditch effort to find "somewhere to put the student" for an hour every day.

Given the cross section of reasons for being in my classes and my determination to teach ALL of them, no matter why they were in the room with me, I established a few rules. In fact, there were only three rules. They went something like this:

1. Be on time, get your work out, and take your seat.
2. Do not talk when I am talking and do not talk the rest of the time either. You have work to do.
3. Remember your competition is you.

The last rule sounded the easiest to them, but it was the most important. The students were welcome to appreciate the efforts of their classmates, but they were not permitted to compare their work to that done by anyone else. I refused to be a part of any of that nonsense.

They signed on for a class that had no textbooks or formal study guides. They sat in a class that required them to participate by "bringing out the answers for each assignment from within themselves" That was how they were expected to meet all the lesson's objectives. Their artistic expressions had to be theirs alone. So, why should anyone else's efforts matter?

My evaluations intentionally pitted them against themselves. And, every time I assigned a new project I moved their individual "goal bars" higher. It was through nurturing their imaginations that they came to visualize and honor the potentials of the world within themselves.

Their results never stopped amazing me; but their results

routinely astounded them. The students created work they never thought they had the talents to do. They knew I believed in them. In turn, they believed in themselves; they just took off with the idea. To a person (and some of you reading this could be former students), they all achieved. They all became more then they thought they could be. However, in reality, they all became exactly who they could be. It was marvelous and sometimes miraculous as well. They all believed.

That is what believing is all about. It is reaching our highest capabilities, working to pull from within ourselves the potentials just waiting for our call. Believe that you can and you will. Jesus of Nazareth often said,

"As you believe so shall it be."

No one can justify disputing that logic.

Consider Glenn Cunningham who was his own competition both on and off the track. His goal was placing first at the finish line. By believing that he could, he did. He finished first at the finish line of life.

Consider Betsy who believed she could live a rich, rewarding life. She joyfully wheeled herself right into all of it. Glenn and Betsy set their own high bars to reach their achievements. Their dreams were big, but they believed, and lived to delight in the fulfillments of their dreams. As they believed so it was.

Consider the Roebling family and the persistence with which they fought on and on and on. Until at last, the great span not only stood, it has stood for decades, and with God's grace it will stand for decades more. The Brooklyn Bridge is a New York City landmark, as well as a major wedge in the city's transportation system. Firm beliefs in dreams bring successes.

When we believe in our dreams and inspirations,
when we believe in ourselves,
when we believe that we are here
on Spaceship Earth by divine design,
when we realize and
accept the miracles that we are…
then nothing is impossible,
nothing.
Believe in your dreams.

A TRAGIC NOTE:

WASHINGTON AUGUSTUS ROEBLING II WAS the grandson of John Roebling and nephew of Washington A. Roebling. In 1912, he and a close friend toured Europe until early spring. When his friend became ill, he sailed home early.

31-year old Roebling euphorically boarded the Titanic at Southampton as a First Class passenger in April. On the night of April 14th, he helped load the lifeboats, reassuringly telling all those he assisted that they would be back on board the Titanic very soon. Then from the lifeboats, they watched in horror as he and the others on the ship became unfortunate victims on that fateful night.

Washington was the only son of Charles Roebling. His father sponsored the rebuilding of the west wall of the Trinity Episcopal Church in Philadelphia in his son's honor. However, he never recovered from the loss of Washington. Charles Roebling died in 1918 at the age of 69 from Bright's disease and a broken heart. His wife had preceded him in death, dying in 1903, when Washington was still a child.

14

Being Believable

Walk the path of your dreams.

BE BELIEVABLE. BELIEVE IN YOURSELF and the power beyond, within, and around you. Apart from that critical thought, there is more to believing than just you and your beliefs. How you relate to your "Fellow Miracles" is important, too. Needless to say you are not living on this planet all by yourself. How you appear to others, how you treat others, what you say to others, and what you contribute in support of others, those actions count, too.

Here is an account that supports that point.

Working with my Russian counterparts, I helped coordinate the founding of the first two private schools in the history of the USSR. The year the activities for those projects began was 1989. That was the year classes officially started at the first school, which was called Dom Stankevich. The second school, The Soviet (now Slavic) Anglo American School "Marina," followed in 1991. Their start-ups occurred during the tenures of Mikhail Gorbachev and Boris Yletsin, before the break-up of the USSR and the birth of today's Russian Federation.

Returning in later September of 1989 from my first trip to Moscow, I was met by my son, Steve, and my Mother at the airport. It was still the era of the KGB. The Iron Curtain still hung across parts of Europe. The middle of Berlin was still divided by a fortified wall. Needless to say my family was relieved and happy to see me.

On the ride home from the airport, I inquired about my waiting phone messages. The two quickly glanced at each other. Then one of them replied, "You can check them when you get home."

Once in the house and settled, I went to the message machine to see why they had given me such a curious response to my earlier question. The messages seemed routine until a woman with a slightly southern accent came on with this message, "Elaine, this is Brenda's mother. I am calling to tell you that Brenda is dead. She was murdered in Tennessee. They don't know who did it, but we didn't bring her back to Ohio."

She paused to compose herself, and then she slowly continued, "You might not have known, but she had been living in Tennessee and was getting along pretty good. She was happy there. So that's where we buried her."

Then in a softer voice, she added, "Brenda always spoke so highly of you. She used to talk about the things you had said to her. She appreciated the time you spent with her when she was in the hospital. We knew you'd want to know what happened to her. She never forgot you, Elaine. So, we wanted to thank you, and… and to let you know."

Then the woman, identified only as Brenda's mother hung up the receiver.

There is no question the message was meant for me. The woman called me by my first name. She had looked up my phone number, which was coded in the directory with only my first and middle initials. I could hear the heartbreak in the voice of the devastated mother who called me. Sadly, at that very moment I did not recall Brenda.

I have overcome several serious health issues during my lifetime. As it turned out, 22 years earlier Brenda had been my hospital roommate for a week. At that time I was 21-years old. Brenda was about my age. She had led a troubled life. She asked a lot of questions about believing and how to make choices and live in faith. We talked about how she might go about redirecting her life. That time in the hospital is how Brenda remembered me.

Nonetheless, the point of this recount is that you never know what your influences are, or will be, on others. You never know when what you say or do will impact the lives of other Brenda's, others who will believe in and remember you. As you move through life, you naturally expect that the footprints you leave in the sand will just gradually wash out to sea. However, sometimes people who follow will walk in those footprints, just as Brenda walked in mine.

At any moment, a "Brenda" could be sitting or standing next to you. Then you will be the one who leaves footprints in the sand for that person to follow. By your words, actions, and demeanor you could be a life-long influence on another person. That is powerful. You could be "the someone" they will believe in. And, you might never know.

During my at-home convalescence from the illness when I met Brenda, there were occasions when poetry came to me spontaneously. Ironically one of the writings swirled back into my mind as I was developing this chapter. Its author is really not I, but the poem reflects what has been presented. I offer it to you.

Believe in yourself
In the things that you do.
For those who are weak
Will lean upon you.

Endeavor each day
A good example to be.
Others pattern their lives
After what they see.

Know what you believe
In the depths of your heart.

So when you are questioned
You'll gladly impart.

In all life, its living,
You will never go far
Until you know deep within
Just who you are.

Believe in yourself.

Those words spilled out magically across a yellow legal pad off the end of my pencil one evening, as I lay in bed too weak to lift a spoon to my mouth. I have kept the poem all these years, never knowing why. Now I know why. Although it was for me then, it is for you now.

As you see, we are never alone. From the very beginning that was never the plan. With our well-timed lives on Earth we receive encouragement and we bring encouragement and hope and motivation to others who walk with us. It bears remembering, in fact never forgetting, what the power of believing can bring to you and likewise to others. Some call those times "gifts." Others know them as "miracles." In any event, they are often exactly what is needed, exactly when it is needed.

A person who consciously, but in many instances unknowingly, influenced the lives of countless others was Vince Lombardi (1913-1970). The legendary football player, coach of the Green Bay Packers in the 1960's, and football executive, serves as an example of a man who lived, as he believed.

Lombardi was a strong-willed man whose influences still echo across the bleachers of stadiums and bounce off the walls of locker rooms around this nation. With his direction the Green Bay Packers won the first two Super Bowls in 1966 and 1967. The

Super Bowl trophy is named in Lombardi's honor. As a head coach in the National Football League, he never had a losing season. But, those recognitions and achievements say only a scant about just what a faith-filled, decent man he was.

Raised in Brooklyn, New York, Lombardi lived through cruel abuse and rampant racial discrimination as a child of Italian immigrants. Consequently, he tolerated no discrimination among his players. He made it crystal clear to all his teams that people's givens were acceptable. Acceptance would not be predicated on social status, race, religion, sexual orientation, or the person's last name. He said that if he ever learned any one of his players had mistreated a fellow teammate with discrimination,

He would be off the team
before his butt ever hit the ground.

And Lombardi meant it. The three constants in Lombardi's life were sports, family, and faith. As an adult, he made an effort to take communion every day. On believing and achieving dreams Lombardi once said,

We would accomplish more things
if we did not think of them as impossible.

Vince Lombardi accomplished great things. But then, he did not consider any of his dreams to be impossible, nor should we.

Over 2000 years ago, a man named Jesus walked on this earth. And as he said many times,

As you have believed,
so it will be done unto you.

Sometimes we forget that Jesus not only came to spread the word of everlasting life, but he also came to change people's expectations of how they spent their Earthly lives. Jesus assured them they were all one, all parts of a much larger Whole. He reminded them they were all the children of God.

However, Jesus also advised his listeners that if they believed they could look fear in the eye. He encouraged them to feel joyous and confident. If they believed nothing was beyond their grasp they could be free. And so it is for all of us as well. If we believe, we *are* free.

Jesus' miracles not only healed suffering, they were symbolic. He opened the eyes of the blind so they could see truth. He brought strength to the legs of the crippled so they could walk in the light. He released the tongues of the dumb so they could sing praises and rejoice. The lame, ill, and obsessed all realized the freedoms and joys of his miracles because they believed. Mary Magdalene walked from Magdala to the shores of the Sea of Galilee in search of Jesus because she believed he could expel the demons from her mind. And, he did. *"As you have believed, so it will be done unto you."*

It bears repeating, we are all one. We have the strength of many to support and underpin us on Earth and the energy of the Universe to surround us. We can feel empowered and energized if we believe in the Power beyond, within, and around us.

Consider the beliefs of Glenn Cunningham, R. Buckminster Fuller, and John, Emily, and Washington Roebling. Your dreams are just as possible as theirs. Your dreams hold the potential for you to make your life and your world a better place. If your dreams were not to be yours, they would have never been placed in your heart. Walk the Pathways of your dreams.

Before turning to the next chapter titled Pathways allow me to recap several points.

1. You have untapped powers waiting to work within and around you.
2. As an eternal soul, a one-of-a-kind miracle, you have the potential to affect the lives of people who will live 100's of years from today.
3. It is reasonable to consider that you can influence the lives of people who will never forget what you said to them, even if you do not remember what you said.
4. In those times, the message is not *about* the deliverer, it is *for* the listener.
5. You start life with nothing, save your first inhaled breath of the spirit from God. You leave your Earthbound life with nothing, save your last exhale.
6. Between the start and the finish of your tenure, you have the opportunity to live an inspiring, miraculous, upbeat life.
7. Other travelers, whose journeys mix and mingle with yours in remarkable ways, surround you.
8. Believing, determination, and joy are keys to making your life all you dream it to be.
9. Be transformed by the renewing of your mind.
10. Become what you believe.

15

PATHWAYS

Be the light others want to stand next to.

As you know, your unique life goes appreciably deeper than "just" living. On unfathomable levels you are conscious of your Pathways, your unparalleled life's journeys, your contracts with the Source, the Universe, God. That said, it should be kept in mind:

» You are accountable for the lesson plans you brought with you to Earth.

» Your soul is aware of your obligation to fulfill your destiny.

» When you keep in touch with your higher self your predestined Pathways unfold before you.

» You instinctively know your lifetime has definite purpose and meaning.

» How you address your goals is your decision.

» Freewill affords you the choice to actively proceed or regress and do nothing.

America's canon of free verse poetry, Walt Whitman wrote lovely contemplative thoughts on life and its meaning. In the last verses of his introspective poem *The Child asked, What is the grass?* Whitman wrote about what is to become of us,

What do you think has become
of the young and old men?
What do you think has become

of the women and children?
They are alive and well somewhere;
The smallest sprouts show
there is really no death,
And if ever there was
it led forward life,
and does not wait at the end
to arrest it,
And ceased the moment life appeared.
All goes onward and outward...
and nothing collapses,
And to die is different from
what any one supposed,
and luckier.

How true. *"All goes onward and outward... and nothing collapses."* As Whitman so aptly penned, *"nothing collapses."* Everything returns to what it has always been. In the blink of eons your Earth time tenure concludes and you move on *"from what any one supposed, and luckier."*

Between birth and death you walk your Pathways. At times your Pathways will loom clear and unobstructed before you. On those occasions you sprint with exhilaration along high, wind swept, sun-dazzled trails that you hope will go on forever. Other times your Pathways could pass through baffling, somber, and on occasion nightmarish places. Or your Pathways become misted in a haze that clingingly surrounds you in its veil, confusing and slowing your pace. In all cases, your Pathways are designed to guide you home. Eight ideas, cautions, and suggestions to consider in support of your journey are proposed on the following pages. Fine-tuning your mind, emotions, and goals helps you stay the course.

In the best of scenarios, we easily travel our Pathways toward the one eternal light, the Universe, our God, the Source. However, the routes differ for each of us. They are based on the obligations of our lesson plans, the goals that support the soul's Earth time evolutionary experiences.

We hold separate agendas so the suggestions offered might not all be appropriate for you. Yet, being aware of them could assist you with another "Miracle" seeking guidance to move toward his or her Pathway, someone like "my" Brenda.

Pathway ideas include:

1. Identify what you "want"
2. Believe in your self worth
3. Be engaged in your life
4. Push out negatives
5. Trust your experiences
6. Take full responsibility
7. Toss away limiting thoughts
8. Establish a belief system

The above is a personal checklist. Let them serve as springboards as you develop your own list.

1. Identify what it is you "want."

Using a road map or a navigation system is a fairly dependable way to get where you want to go. As with most journeys, a variety of roads allow you the luxury of some flexibility. You can zip along a 6-lane super highway with restricted access and limited rest stop areas. You can meander country blacktops, pulling over to pick wild flowers or to enjoy a picnic at a scenic overlook. No matter the route you elect, as long as you keep to your Pathways and/or intentions many roads will eventually guide you to your destination.

Identifying what you "want" in your life is akin to planning a road trip. First you decide where you want to go. Then you study a map to locate its actual site, the destination. With your target established, you start to plan your route. Your intention is to reach your goal. That is your ultimate focus.

Now, compare the road trip and its navigation options to identifying what it is that you "want" in your life, where you want to go. What you "want" does not mean you know *how* you will get what you want. It *does* mean you have decided and/or identified a "want." You have a goal. A destination is in your mind.

A universal law (Sometimes called the power of intention.) says you bring to yourself what you are, and what you intend to receive. Therefore, you must drive in the direction of your intention or you will end up lost, endlessly wandering. Being on the right road will take you to your destination.

If you have misgivings about a road trip, you generally decide not to go. If you have misgivings about your wants, then your misgivings will assume the leadership role. They will cancel your goal. You will end up with a "want" that forever stays what it initially was, just a "want." Be determined about the Pathways you choose. You must believe to receive.

A simple suggestion is to write your "wants" on a piece of paper, so you can look at the list from time to time. Hold those wants as intentions that you believe you are going to receive, drive toward. Remember the power of positivity. It may not always appear as such, but optimism reigns supreme in this world of ours. Just as you optimistically pack for a trip, optimistically look forward to achieving your wants, you dreams, your intentions.

Years ago I started the habit of jotting what I wanted on a Post-it note and sticking it on the side of my refrigerator. My wants were private and personal. They were not topics for discussion, so I stuck the paper out of the range of people's vision. I never mentioned the list to anyone. The desires were just mine, for me. My paper could have one entry or several. Over the years my wants have been "all over the map." Some would have seemed frivolous or self-serving to other people, but they were what I wanted at the time. As each item became a reality, I paused, looked up, and said, "Thank you." (We all enjoy being appreciated. God likes that, too.) Then I crossed it off the list.

In the fall of 1988, I entered a want that read, "Travel to Europe." I had never visited Europe and decided I wanted to see what the world looked like on the other side of the Atlantic Ocean. I did not target a country, and I did not have any money saved for a trip. I just wanted to go abroad. That want took a decidedly unexpected turn.

Six months later, in March of 1989, I received a letter from Glasgow, Scotland. It came as a surprise because I did not know anyone in Scotland. I still do not know anyone in Scotland. The handwritten letter covered 13 pages and was signed by a woman named Alla. As it turned out, that letter heralded the start of my association with the Soviets in Moscow, Russia, USSR. The letter explained that they were seeking my educational expertise and support as they started the first private school in the history of their country. The school would be named "Children's Courses in English Literature, History, and Social Studies" at Dom Stankevich.

A few words of explanation:

I mentioned the Dom Stankevich/House of Stankevich project earlier. Nikolai Stankevich (1813-1840) was a poet-philosopher who once lived in the house chosen for the school. As an early 19th Century writer and advocate for education, his former home became a historically significant site for the first educational cooperative in the USSR. Dom Stankevich received its official license to proceed with its plan in 1987.

The length of the title reflected Gorbachev's orders that it could not be officially called a "school." The USSR already had schools, so this first effort at private education had to use the longer title. Today it continues at its original site. Its staff enriches and supplements children's educational experiences with bi-weekly lessons in English and culturally related tours to foreign countries. Now, back to the story.

I later learned that in February of 1989 a Russian educator named Alla had attended a conference somewhere in Europe. At that conference she handed her letter for me to a Scotsman. He promised to mail it as soon as he returned to Glasgow. He carried it back to Glasgow and dutifully posted it. During the years of The Cold War, sending a letter from the USSR destined for the USA was no easy feat. It could only get out of Moscow safely if someone hand carried it and mailed it from a free country. The rest of the story about the start-up months and ensuing years spent helping my Soviet (now Russian Federation) co-administrators successfully establish the first and second private learning facilities in Moscow would be another entire book. Suffice it is to say, and keeping to the point of this first section, I received that which I intended I wanted. I certainly "Travel(ed) to Europe."

If you act on the suggestion to write your "wants" on a Post-it note, keep in mind you are dealing with God. He sees your list. And he is all you are and more. Therefore, if you know you possess a good sense of humor, or you can put entertaining spins on circumstances, think again and get prepared. Consider what happened with my want to "Travel to Europe." In 1988, I pictured misty London, glittering Paris, or time-honored Rome. I never considered my first trip to Europe would include the glistening wetness of cold, drizzly, late September days in the USSR's monolithic city of Moscow.

Since September of 1989, I have visited Europe on multiple occasions and traveled to Russia perhaps 18-plus times. Each trip to Moscow has included interactions with Russian educators and their students. My want on the Post-it note pivoted into a totally unexpected, once-in-a-lifetime, completely unforeseen adventure. What an incredible opportunity. One I continue to enjoy.

Recall for a moment earlier examples of individuals like John Roebling and the steel rope he patented well over 20 years before the inspiration for the Brooklyn Bridge came to him.

The Brooklyn Bridge is still suspended by steel wire cables. Roebling's ideas and those of all the others came solely to them. Consider the revelations and discoveries for which they had been unknowingly prepared. Over the years leading up to the visits of their inspirations each one of them had learned what they would need to know.

It was uncanny in my case as well. The Russians knew nothing about me, except for my name and home address, and that I was involved in education in the United States. However, my background included advanced educational degrees and hands-on experience teaching and supervising children and teachers in all grades K-12. I had administrative experience in developing and instituting curriculum and monitoring special pilot programs, training and evaluating teachers, managing budgets, working with parents, and modeling classroom techniques. All those skills were critical for the tasks at hand in Moscow. The realization of my "want" was in fact the actualization of who I was and still am.

In reflection, for two previous decades many of the Pathways I chose were leading directly to the challenges I faced working with the Russians. And, yes, it was another of the Universe's single call outs. I was the sole American initially invited to assist with the start-up developments of those first, two, cutting edge schools. So, be prepared. Your "want" could bring you a lifetime of adventure and enrichment beyond your wildest dreams. And, as my "Travel to Europe" desire might have seemed frivolous at the time, look how it evolved. It became an international collaboration filled with on-going successes and benefits for many, many people.

What matters with your Post-it note list is that you stay alert, flexible, and maintain your sense of humor. Watch the horizon for the emergence of the "want" in the distance. You can never be sure when your desire will approach or when you will become more of who you are than you think you are. Allowing what you want is not illegal, immoral, indecent, or out-of-print you will typically receive what your heart desires and more. Just stay optimistic and hopeful about receiving it. Be patient. It is the Universe you are dealing with out there, time is only on this side of your total eternal existence.

In the meantime, prepare to do serious work toward your want. After the initial contacts, on the front end of the development of the schools, I spent many days planning, organizing, developing teacher training presentations, reviewing curriculum, and ordering and shipping English language textbooks to Moscow. Since shipping into the USSR was no easy feat in 1989, I called a man I thought should know how to do it. I was correct. Armand Hammer offered me the best advice for safely getting the materials delivered to Moscow. Everything but atlases and English dictionaries arrived at their destination.

Your respect for yourself and the ultimate appreciation and realization of your efforts bestows priceless gifts upon you and upon your world.

2. Believe in your self worth.

You live with the abundance of the Universe at your fingertips. You have the privilege and opportunity to enjoy all of it. You have a Post-it note tacked some place to remind you of your intentions. And you are ready for your "wants" to begin appearing. Life is sure to become, or will continue to be, a wonder filled adventure for you.

However, as alluded to in the previous section, having a solid belief in your want does not automatically guarantee that your intention will be magically handed to you. Take into account that on the other side of just one breath there is no such thing as time. So snapping your fingers for quick results and immediate service is not going to influence the pacing or the arrival of your desire one bit. Time operates in the Earth realm. It assists mankind with organization. Sun-moon, seasons, and day-night sequences support the passing of time lest we forget a birthday or an appointment. It will not matter at all if you express impatience or discontent. Neither is "of" the other side. Take into consideration that you are made of particles over 13 billion years old. A few days, weeks, months, or even years are nothing to the Universe.

So, once the list is "taped to the side of the refrigerator" you still have more to do. It would be unwise to sit back, relax, and idly wait. Intentionally cited in earlier chapters were examples of many who believed in their self-worth and realized their seemingly impossible dreams. However, their dreams materialized through hard work, determination, positive attitudes, and by the grace of God. Look back on the agonizing struggle to reach success experienced by Glenn Cunningham. He learned to walk again on legs so badly mutilated by a fire that the doctors wanted to amputate them. My friend Betsy dealt with creating a rewarding life for herself from the seat of a wheelchair. Glenn and Betsy both diligently worked and believed in their wants and their self worth.

Thomas Edison held fast to his strong sense of self worth. However he also subscribed to the power of hard work and determination. He did not invent the very first light bulb, but he believed he could invent an incandescent light bulb that would burn brightly and for longer periods of time. He tested hundreds of different filaments to find the perfect match to his needs. He repeated and repeated and repeated his efforts until at last one finally worked. He patented his "New Type Edison Lamp" in 1880. The basic shape has changed little since its inception.

The famous spiritual leader Siddhartha Gautama Buddha taught about self worth. (The word "Buddha" is not a name. It is a title that translates to "awakened one.") Gautama lived between 563-483 BC. His father was the Hindu king of an ancient republic in the Himalayan foothills. He confined Prince Gautama to the family palace until he was in his late 20's, so he would remain undefiled by the world. He wanted his son to become the next king.

At 29-years of age, Gautama escaped the palace to take a look at his future subjects. When he entered the *real* world he saw it in all its nakedness. For the first time in his protected life he saw disease, suffering, death, and unfulfilled needs. He determined to study and become an enlightened teacher in an effort to help and heal his countrymen. This introspective quote by Gautama is typical of the founder of Buddhism. It represents his belief in the value of self worth.

You can search
throughout the entire universe
for someone who is more deserving
of your love and affection
than you are yourself,
and that person
is not to be found anywhere.
You, yourself,
as much as anybody
in the entire universe,
deserve your love and affection.

To love one's self because you deserve *"your love and affection"* allows you to freely extend love to others. The truth is, if you love yourself and feel self worth then you are at peace and less likely to hurt others. Loving yourself is not akin to being egotistical. Egotism is a negative personality trait. It indicates tendencies to show off and be extremely self-occupied. To Gautama Buddha's way of thinking,

If your compassion
does not include yourself,
it is incomplete.

He encouraged his followers to always be compassionate toward themselves. You should always be compassionate and kind toward yourself as well.

Gautama Buddha strongly believed in the power of one. He

cautioned against blaming others for your circumstances. That is a defeatist tactic. You are accountable to one. That one is you. He wrote,

No one saves us
but ourselves,
no one can
and no one may.
We ourselves
must walk the path… .

When you *"walk the path(ways)"* of your life's purposes keep your self-esteem with you. A sense of self worth, which is a healthy combination of emotions and beliefs, allows you to be confident, optimistic, and kinder toward others. It can be exhilarating to know you are accepted, loved, and respected by society. Feeling a personal acceptance, love, and respect for yourself is healthy, positive, and a high priority as well.

Your visit to Earth is intentional. You brought special interests, talents, and skills with you. No matter if you captain a ship, saw lumber, teach students, weave rugs, bake brownies, lay pavement, sell automobiles, preach sermons, check pulses, chair a corporation, rope horses, drive taxis… whatever you do, do it well. Work with pride. Use your God given gifts positively. Maintain your self worth at all cost. What you contribute and why you are here are both important facets of you.

Two clarifications are in order:

1. A sense of positive self worth cannot be equated to blatant full-blown vanity, egotism, narcissism, or conceit. Those negative personality traits gnaw at your soul. Unlike pure love for yourself, they indicate overt cravings for

attention, unrealistic senses of superiority, and obnoxious self-centeredness. They do not hold rank with a solid sense of self worth.

2. Sincere humility and humbleness are virtues. Demeaning self-degradation, personal flagellation, and false humility lead others to see you as less than you truly are. You are a miracle. That is an honor to be worn with pride.

Buddha advocated that his devotees should believe in their self worth. No matter your creed or religious affiliation, believing in your self worth is critical to achieving success in your lifetime's experiences. Honor the miraculous soul embedded in you.

3. Be engaged in your life.

The zest for living wanes, shrivels, and can even die when you are not passionate about what you "want," what you enjoy, and what you do with your time. This section encourages you to be passionately engaged in building your life. Love, love, love your life. Siddhartha Gautama Buddha taught that mankind should overcome doubt and live in the moment. He believed that today supersedes both the previous day and tomorrow. Stay in the present. Pay attention to what is before you. With each dawn comes rebirth, the new you, and a Pathway waits for your footsteps.

Be aggressively active about doing and going and being as you build your life. Do not just live your life. Keep the positive forces of enthusiasm and happiness flowing into and through yourself. And, let laughter be a part of every day. Charlie Chaplin used to say,

A day without a laugh is a wasted day.

Chaplin's pitiful, pain filled, wretched, growing up years were shared in an earlier chapter of this book. His resiliency and positive outlook is worth repeating, *"A day without a laugh is a wasted day."* If you cannot find something amusing about the day, pull something out of your memory bank that entertained you in the past. If it seemed priceless then, it can make your heart sing or bring a smile to your face again. It matters to stay upbeat and filled with happiness, so do it!

In actuality, you possess all you need to enhance your engagement on Spaceship Earth. That includes not only social and active experiences, but it includes peace filled and serene times as well. Sprinkle variety into your days. Too much of one thing is too much. In the 18th Century, the British poet and well-known hymnodist William Cowper (1731-1800) observed,

Variety is the very spice of life,
that gives it all its flavor.

Cowper's quote is an appropriate reminder. Enhance your life with sprinklings of spice. In the process of opening the doors to variety and flexibility, you will live longer, be happier, and be blessed with more gratifying adventures.

The channeling mystic and author Sanaya Roman writes in her books about conversations with her spiritual guide, Orin. According to Roman, he believes you have everything you need within yourself to have a productive life. One message from Orin reads,

…the universe is friendly,
that it is unlimited in its abundance,
that everything is happening perfectly
for our good
although we may not always
understand why,
and that we can
choose to grow through joy
rather than through struggle.

Roman's practice is to interact with her mystical guide Orin. Then she shares his wisdom. For some folks paranormal forces are uncomfortable to consider. However Orin's message cannot be expressed more forthrightly. *"…that everything is happening perfectly for our good."* Remember, it is about the message, not the messenger.

While the high end of the teeter-totter on this subject has you actively engaged in your life, on the ground the other end of the teeter-totter could be labeled,

The world owes me a living.

As discussed previously, it is your responsibility to be responsible for yourself to build your life. If you tend to spend a considerable amount of your time in an inert state of unhappiness, well that *is* a problem but that is *your* problem. Waiting around or saturating yourself with senseless worry or trumped up blame stalls you. It steals your joy. It destroys your power. You are a miracle on a mission. Keep your power.

The American entrepreneur, inventor, and co-founder of Apple Inc., Pixar, and NeXT Inc., Steve Jobs kept his power. He understood the limitations of time on Earth and the necessity to collect all the gold rings he could as he rode the merry-go-round of life. He kept all things in a clear perspective. He was also aware of the danger of feeling trapped by the opinions of others. He believed that,

Your time is limited,
so don't waste it
living someone else's life.
Don't be trapped by dogma…
which is living with the results

of other people's thinking.
Don't let the noise of others' opinions
drown out your own inner voice.
And most important,
have the courage to follow
your heart and intuition.

Jobs, like R. Buckminster Fuller, most definitely had *"the courage to follow his heart and intuition."* He did not allow *"the noises of others' opinions"* to determine who his *"inner voice"* told him he could be. He persisted in following the Pathways to his dreams.

Steve Jobs lost consciousness the day before he died. He lingered in a coma from the complications of pancreatic cancer, which had been diagnosed in 2003. On October 5, 2011, at age 56, right before he passed he opened his eyes. He stared at each member of his family tenderly, deeply, and intentionally. Then his gaze moved up and over their shoulders. His last words were,

Oh wow! Oh wow! Oh wow!

"Oh wow!" and then he was gone. What did Steve Jobs see? Perhaps the Universe from which we have all come. On many levels Jobs was a man to be respected, a man who enthusiastically engaged himself in his life and his life's work. He stands as a miraculous human being who saw opportunities and said, "Yes!" Steve Jobs was to the 21st Century what R. Buckminster Fuller was to the 20th Century. They singlehandedly made differences in the lives of millions of people on this planet called Earth by acting on their inspirations.

Once I cautiously climbed the dark, narrow, winding, metal stairs to the very top of the outside of the dome on St. Isaac's Cathedral in St. Petersburg, Russia. Another time I hung on tightly as I bounced happily along in a motor-driven dugout tree, turned canoe, up the brisk-running headwaters of the Amazon River in Ecuador. Lots of times I have made my favorite macaroon pie, volunteered as a Sunday church school teacher, chewed a fresh stick of gum, and dined on a sizzling sirloin steak. Each of those experiences brought me joy. I had fun with the momentous events and enjoyed the no-reason-to-write-home, inconsequential, everyday happenings, too.

The point to be made is, stay engaged in your life. It does not matter what you are doing. Be in the moment. The "doing" is what matters, not the magnitude or monumentally of what you do. Be in the moment when you pull on your socks, squeeze toothpaste on your toothbrush, butter an ear of corn, look into the eyes of a child, watch the gentle circling of a hawk, hold someone's hand, whatever you are doing, be consciously engaged.

See, touch, taste, smell, and hear all the minutes of your days and your years. You are gifted with those senses so they can protect you and bring you joy. Use them to stay alert and actively engaged in building your life. Let your passion for living reign supreme.

4. Push out negatives.

Who has not made mistakes? Mistakes provide avenues to arrive at better understandings. They offer opportunities to learn. Mistakes are not always destructive. They are not always a waste of time. Nor are they invariably unfortunate incidents meant to cause shame or blame. Edison learned during his struggles with the light bulb that mistakes could generate the best learning curves in the world. For exactly that same reason, my art students used erasers. And I cautioned them to sketch their first pencil lines lightly so they would be easier to erase as needs arose. The students learned from their mistakes. Their mistakes helped them become better artists.

An erased image, once the lines are removed, is gone. That is the end of it. Your mistakes, once they have passed, are behind you as well. Mistakes are not part of your life so you can keep looking over your shoulder. Nothing can be gained from revisiting what no longer is. Let your mistakes be what they were and are. They were learning curves at the time. Now they are gone.

Giving permission to your past to overwhelm your present in any arena of your life gets you nowhere but stuck in that gutter Oscar Wilde mentioned when he wrote,

We are all in the gutter,
but some of us are looking at the stars.

Earlier in this book the topics of optimism and pessimism were sufficiently addressed. A case was made for why it is better to live with a song in your heart than with a groan in your throat. Your soul does best when you bring it joy. Remember Lew's Laws for healing when he had cancer? Your physical body does best when you fill it with joy. Love, laughter, positive outlooks, thinking good thoughts, performing good deeds, whatever it takes, always stay on the bright side of the street. Walk in the light. Intentionally surround yourself with others whose outlooks on life are positive, encouraging, and full of energy. As you know, it can be life threatening to do otherwise.

However several observations about people who could be part of your life ought to be addressed. Every person is not a favorable individual with whom you should spend large amounts of time. For reasons known only on higher levels than ours, individuals do exist who seem by nature to be jealous, narrow, nasty, envious, and mean spirited. (I would guess that if they realized how powerfully dangerous their negative thoughts could be they might not work so hard at being disgruntled.) However, it cannot be your life's goal or responsibility to drag them kicking and screaming to the table of hope and happiness.

Change only comes from a desire within the person. Forcing change upon someone is ultimately a futile attempt at uninvited reconstruction, a waste of your time and efforts. Individuals in negative mindsets will spring back into their well-worn tracks of lament as quickly as they leave your presence. So save yourself the disappointment. If you want to, need to, or must be around gloom-and-doomers, remember to always be who you are. Do not "be" who they are. And when you are in their company do not give them permission to chip away at your self worth or optimism.

You returned to Earth to "experience" life. You knew there would be sad and luckless and wearisome days tucked in with all the other more welcoming ones. Negative experiences will and do come to you. Inevitabilities in life are deaths, illnesses, accidents, heartaches, disappointments, slanders, and difficult spans of time. Undeniably they can dash you to the rocks. That being acknowledged, when those times happen, be mindful that you are not alone. In a Universe this full of vibrancy, this full of generosity, this full of love, you are not alone at all.

The Universe teems with auspiciousness and energy. The ability to tap into that affirming power is yours to call upon whenever you need it. Use it to retool your emotions and your life, to get back on the Pathways to your goals. You owe it to yourself, to your soul, to your passions, and to your dreams to move forward.

A favorite poem of the professional golfer, Arnold Palmer (1929-) is this popular one. Here are three of its six stanzas,

If you think you are beaten, you are;
If you think that you dare not, you don't;
If you'd like to win, but you don't think you can,
It's almost a chinch you won't.

If you think you'll lose, you've lost;
For out in the world you'll find
Success begins with a fellow's will;
It's all in the state of mind.

Life's battles don't always go
To the stronger or faster man,
But sooner or later the man who wins
Is the man who thinks he can.

A little known, late 19th Century, writer named Walter D. Wintle penned that encouraging piece titled *Thinking*. Palmer must have memorized every line of Wintle's poem. Considered to be one of the finest golfers in the history of the men's sport, he holds the acclaimed titles of seven major championship tournaments. He was inducted into the World Golf Hall of Fame in 1974. An honorable man, Palmer practiced and played hard, but he won because he thought he could. The power in staying positive leads to greater lifetime experiences on all levels.

Irrefutably your attitude is *"all in the state of (your) mind."* You can look at an apple pie as half eaten or still half there. You can complain that your shoe is too tight or look across the room at someone who has no leg. You can see the glory in the morning or complain that you have to go to work or school. You have choices. You can bemoan or be merry, lament or let go. *"It's all in the state of (your) mind."*

Gary Zukav (1942-), the author of *The Seat of the Soul*, discusses complaining in his best seller. Zukav considers complaining to be an action taken when you do not want to be held accountable. He writes,

Complaining is a form of manipulation
...for example, (it) is exactly that dynamic of
wanting someone to be responsible
for what you experience,
and to fix things for you.

Zukav believes complaining opens an avenue that causes you to relinquish you power. Complaining announces to the world that someone else has taken charge of you and your life in whatever venue. There is no joy in complaining.

Keep what matters in the headlights as you travel the Pathways toward your dreams. Keep to the high roads. Focus on your "wants," your goals, and the road ahead. If you start looking around for someone to blame or (worse yet) drive focused on the past by looking in the rearview mirror, you will hit every pothole in the pavement. You might as well park the car before you slam into a tree. You are never going to get where you want to go.

In support of staying optimistic, in *The New Testament's* book of Philippians 4:8 it reads,

Finally, brothers and sisters,
whatever is true,
whatever is noble,
whatever is right,
whatever is pure,
whatever is lovely,
whatever is admirable—
if anything is excellent or praiseworthy—
think about such things.

"If anything is excellent or praiseworthy think about such things." Flush your mind of judgmental negatives, past regrets, and debasing internal conversations that sadden your heart and wound your soul. Let loses, mistakes, and uncomfortable issues stay where they happened. Seek forgiveness from others and allow yourself to be forgiven. Then move on.

Do not carry unnecessary baggage. Remember the grumbling woman at the airport who carried the overflowing tapestry bag?

She was accustomed to its weight. She easily hefted it on to and off the plane. That uncanny symbolism should not be overlooked. Her bag overflowed with stuff. Stuff she ably toted, like the weighty attitudes and wrinkled perspectives in her mind, her heart, and her spirit.

In Gary Zukav's book *The Seat of the Soul* he discusses the power of The Golden Rule, which he suggests is a dynamic of karma. He writes,

You receive from the world
what you give to the world.

Give to the world what you want to *"receive from the world."* Intend that which you want to bring to yourself and never let it be negative. After all, you have so much to look forward to enjoying. Looking forward is exactly what you should habitually do.

5. Trust your experiences.

Your experiences differ from out-and-out mistakes. Experiences are true teachers. Some bring incredible joys, some carry warnings, and some are filled with learning tools. No matter, review each situation as it presents itself. Then make any necessary "refolding" adjustments or additions in your suitcase of life and keep moving. Experiences are what they are. Learn from them, understand them, and keep going.

Trust that your experiences come specifically to you. They are designed to lead you closer to the successful completion of your lesson plans. Experiences assume a myriad of forms. Be continually alert as to how they arrive, what forms they take, and the incredible timing they possess. Any and/or all of them can lead to fascinating adventures or awakenings. Some times you happen upon a "chance" encounter. Another time you "accidentally" hear one sentence tucked into an entire discourse that holds very significant information for you. While on another occasion you finally cede to an incessant nudging in your mind. The list goes on. Experiences, multi-faceted as they are, bring messages, miracles, and magic to your life.

As mentioned in a previous section, your interactions with the hundreds of people in your life are critical to building success into your experiences. Mixed into your wealth of influences will be a plethora of different types of people. They will offer you a patchwork quilt of experiences.

Recently my son, Steve, stood in front of a fast food counter in the middle of an afternoon waiting to place his order. The restaurant was nearly empty, save for a few lingering diners and a group of three standing near him. Their orders were being filled. However, none of the wait staff gave my 6'2" son a glance. He watched and remained calm, quiet, polite, albeit a bit confused that he seemed to be invisible to absolutely everyone behind the counter.

At last the manager stepped forward. She surveyed the situation and apologized for her staff's lack of focus. Then she quickly filled Steve's order and added a free pie, a soft drink, an apology, and a smile. That experience does not guarantee you a complimentary dessert and a drink served with a smile every time you remain "civilized" in the face of frustration at a fast food restaurant, but it could! Comfortable times make civility easy. Your tests come when the opposites are the case. Good manners and respectful patience never go out of style. Steve would attest to that.

Unfortunately not everyone you interact with can be counted on to meet your expectations. However, the good news is that most people respond positively to being treated with dignity and respect. Do that. Be respectful, patient, and polite. We are all in this business of "the living souls experience" together. Let civility reign.

When it comes to your relationships with friends and family, circles are good. Consider this visualization. Imagine yourself in the center of your own little universe of relationships. Around you are several rings. Each ring is slightly larger than the one inside it. In each of the rings different individuals stand. None of the circles are beyond your sphere of concern, compassion, or appreciation.

They are your universe of friendships and associations. Nonetheless, the circle closest to you is where the truly trusted and supportive friends and relatives should stand. They are the ones who believe in you, support you, unconditionally love you, give you strength in times of trial, and bring you joy with their presence.

As a word of caution, keep a polite distance, preferably at your outermost circle, for those you loyally care about even though they belittle your dreams and demean your intentions. They might be important to you, but they should not stand too close to you. Even in their own worlds they look for roadblocks first. They openly express fears to proceed, and more often than not they spew their condescension and hopelessness on others. They generally try to transfer their personal misgivings or frustrations about their lives to you and your life. They represent small minds. They steal your energy.

The British-American poet David Whyte (1955-) gave solid succinct advice on critical, dismissive, damaging relationships when he wrote in his poem *Sweet Darkness* that,

...anyone or anything that
does not bring you alive
is too small for you.

In your circles, are there associates who *"bring you alive"* while others are *"too small for you?"* In the company of another, if you do not feel valuable, then they are standing too close to you. They prevent you from breathing the pure air of living. They wound your spirit. They are too small for you. You are blessed as a child of the Universe. Yours is the privilege to grow and become all you can be. No one has the privilege to steal that opportunity from you, to keep you from being alive.

The book of Proverbs is blunt when it speaks about those types. Chapter 6:16-19 says,

There are six things that the Lord hates,
seven that are an abomination to him:
haughty eyes,
a lying tongue,
and hands that shed innocent blood,
a heart that devises wicked plans,
feet that make haste to run to evil,
a false witness who breathes out lies,
and one who sows discord among brothers.

So there it is. Obviously if you have experienced any of the above circumstances you do not stand alone. The list was compiled because somebody had already done some rather ugly things to someone else. There should be some comfort in knowing that in all of man's history you are not the only soul who has experienced the wounding acts of inhumanity. Let us hope you are not guilty of any of the *"abomination(s)"* yourself. On a brighter note there are those who will appreciate, find stimulating, and delight in your aspirations. Let them stand close to you.

Those supportive folks will even help you bring home your dreams. Consider how individuals "make you feel" and you will quickly know where they should stand in your circles of friends and relatives. Should you be unsure, your subconscious, your intuition, always recognizes the differences. Quite simply, one group "beats you up," while the innermost ring makes you feel "upbeat." And in between the inner and outermost circles, there are lots of other rings to accommodate your various relationships.

As for how others "treat" you... . We are all created, but we are not created alike, none of us are the same. So, how can everyone always treat you the way you want to be treated? They cannot and they will not. They have their own lesson plans and work to get done. You have yours. By staying alert and perceptive you will know which people are best to have "circling" the closest around you.

As much as possible stay kind and be civilized toward others. Savor the unlimited numbers of experiences along your Pathways and appreciate their values. Keep your energy up with positive thoughts flowing. You have a wholesome self-worth. You cannot waste time on unnecessary avoidable upsets and divisiveness. Rest assured, God loves you. He knows why you are here. On your super conscious level you know why you are here, too.

6. Take full responsibility.

Webster's dictionary defines responsibility as,

The state or fact of having a duty to deal with
something or of having control over someone.
A moral obligation to behave correctly toward or in respect of…

Aside from your responsibility to your soul and your relationship with the Source, your *"moral obligation"* on Earth is *"to behave correctly toward or in respect of"* yourself. In other words, do your best for yourself and do the best you can to be gentle and caring toward the fellow journeyers you meet along your Pathways.

In only the most deplorable of circumstances are you not responsible for you. About 99% of the time you have an obligation to yourself to be a person who thinks and acts independently and takes full responsibility for both your thoughts and your actions. Doing otherwise signals fear, immaturity, and a conscious desire to be unaccountable to the world.

A man who took complete responsibility for himself and his multiple duties was the 26th President of the United States Theodore "T.R." Roosevelt (1858-1919). Known for his energy, enthusiasm, and his strong leadership qualities, history remembers him as an action-packed and remarkable man. Before becoming President, Roosevelt held numerous positions in the local, state, and federal governments. During his lifetime he was also a rancher, boxer, naturalist, historian, author, hunter, soldier, and the first statesman to be awarded the Nobel Peace Prize. In 1906, he accepted the medal but not the prize money. In 1917, he ordered that the sum of $45,482.83 (Interest had accrued.) be used to provide relief for victims of World War I. During his acceptance speech for the Nobel Peace Prize, which he did not get around to presenting until May 5, 1910, Roosevelt made this comment,

We must ever bear in mind that
the great end in view is righteousness,
justice as between man and man,
nation and nation,
the chance to lead our lives
on a somewhat higher level,
with a broader spirit of
brotherly goodwill one for another.

"The chance to lead our lives on a somewhat higher level" is the rich booming theme of Roosevelt's life-long goal. It was the theme of his Pathways.

His face joins the sculpted portraits of Presidents Abraham Lincoln, Thomas Jefferson, and George Washington on the Mt. Rushmore Memorial in the Black Hills of South Dakota. Along with Thomas Jefferson, Roosevelt is considered to be the best read of all the Presidents. He easily read several books a day and in multiple languages. He also loved poetry. He liked to quote poetry to Robert Frost, one of America's favorite poets. Always direct and clear with his messages, one of Roosevelt's comments on personal responsibility was,

If you could kick the person in the pants
responsible for most of your trouble,
you wouldn't sit for a month.

There is a mountain of truth in that quip. Always accountable for himself and never to be undone, Roosevelt suffered from asthma as a child and late in his life from debilitating inflammatory rheumatism. He died in 1919 from a heart attack at the age of 60. The remark was made that it was probably a blessing Roosevelt died in his sleep, because if he had been awake he would have put up a terrible fight.

All his life Roosevelt assumed responsibility for himself, his actions, and his thoughts. Like him, the responsibility for your life is your obligation. Therein rests a critically important point. When you take full responsibility for yourself there can be no inclination on your part to blame others. As noted earlier, the instant you decide to blame someone else for your problems, you relinquish your power. You release your authority to manage and control your own life. With blame, you broadcast to the world that you are not in charge of you.

The wiser approach is to let mistakes and wrongdoings stay where they occurred. Move away from shameful blaming, accusing, accosting, defaming, and vilifying. None of that besmirching draws you closer to your goal. None of that esteems the noble soul that you are. None of that is worth your valuable time.

Blatant blaming and complaining habits should be erased from your "to do" list. Wayne Dyer discusses unnecessary blame when he speaks to audiences, and he addressed blame in one of his books. Here is his perspective,

All blame is a waste of time.
No matter how much fault

you find with another,
and regardless of how much you blame him,
it will not change you.

Dyer goes on to explain that blame simply takes the focus away from you for a short while as you try to come up with a reason for why you are unhappy or frustrated. Even if you succeed in making another person feel guilty or ashamed, you will have done nothing to change whatever it was about you that made you so unhappy.

Sagaciously the writer George Bernard Shaw observed,

We are made wise
not by the recollection of our past,
but by the responsibility of our future.

You are in charge of you. Period. Hold tight to the reins of personal responsibility.

Lastly, avoid the "but if's." "If," according to Daniel Webster, is a word meaning,

A condition that …, presuming that …, supposing that …,
in the event that… .

By if's usage, "if" is not an indictor that anything can or will happen. With "if" everything is still in limbo. Avoid the necessity to insert uncertainties and doubts into your language and consequently into your life. Be really real. Be authentic.

And, in support of maintaining your center and moving forward, this assurance is offered. You will never control all that life brings to you. Some circumstances and individuals have to be allowed to just be. Make calm, controlled, and thoughtful evaluations when those occasions arise. Let those situations pass through you with as much composure as you can muster. In those periods, listen to your inner voice, your intuitiveness. Your inner being, your spirit, looks out for your best interests. It will assist you in maintaining your full responsibility for you.

7. Toss away limiting thoughts.

Negative thoughts create chemical imbalances in your brain. That is an undisputable medical fact. Additionally, limiting thoughts either tie you where you are or shift you into reverse. This section addresses several "no-no's" that can reap havoc with an otherwise smooth journey.

The kindred fabrications to "but if's" are "should-a," "could-a," and "would-a." They are non-starters and can clutter your Pathways. They will drag you backwards or stall you in your tracks. You can easily find examples of them when you read the newspaper or listen to commentators in the media. Writers and announcers frequently use words that fall into that range. The apprehension they provoke sells real stories mixed with the creation of should-a, could-a, would-a incidents that include imaginary conditions, made-up conclusions, or probabilities that will likely never occur. It can be a major challenge to strain out the truth in articles or on programs where exaggeration and trumped-up terror runs amuck.

You do exactly the same thing to yourself when you launch into "should-a," "could-a," "would-a's" in your mind. When you do that, you pile on the potential negatives. Then, as if looking for validation, you often draw near to an unsuspecting sympathetic ear and voice your misgivings to that warm body.

Pretty soon the non-truths, the figments of your wild imagination have staged a production that no one wants to buy a ticket to see. And, like listening to many of the media representatives in today's world, anyone hearing your trumped-up tale has to dig deeply to locate the threads of truth and separate them from the tangle you have woven and now imagine is true.

"Vicious circle" comes to mind when you limit your thoughts and beliefs. The word "worry" comes to mind as well. Worry is one of the big nets filled with "should-a," "could-a," "would-a's." Whatever word is applied, it is all to no advantage. It damages your chances of being in charge of yourself and your happiness.

"Limiting thoughts" is another bad habit that can consume valuable time. If you are powerless to do anything about something, do not make something up. Focus instead on putting your real and worthy "wants" and dreams on Post-it notes and moving forward along your Pathways. Positive thoughts are the productive ones that count.

Also, avoid making "mental maps" about what is going to happen next. You can no more predict exactly what is going to occur in any future situation than fly without wings and under your own power. Deciding ahead of time how a scene is going to play out should be left to the theater. Oh, you might "get lucky" once in a while, but not enough times to make it a habit. And the result of map-making in your mind is that when you actually have to face reality you often wind up in confusion, shock, anger, or disappointment. The chances are good that things will not go exactly as you had planned them in your thoughts. Do you see what is wrong with that picture?

"Mind reading" also fits into the negative, limiting thoughts category. Unfortunately for the mind reader, what they suppose is more a mirror of them and their thoughts than what the other party is actually thinking. Often you will know when you are speaking with a mind reader. They are the ones who finish your sentences for you. And usually their endings are no way near what yours would have been.

Making "quick judgments and assumptions" about others is another one of those "You should not being doing this" practices. Let circumstances play out, listen, reflect, then consider.

Avoid what is known as "filtering." That is fixating on one fact, one issue, one comment, or one facial expression at the expense of the entire scene. Think globally and with a sense of balanced perspective. Keep an open mind. Let your thoughts stay fluid. Look at the whole picture. Sometimes things are shades of gray, not firmly black or white.

"Over personalization" is another common, unhealthy, limiting, social trait. It might come as a shock, but everything is not always about you. Every story is not a springboard for your story. Every comment is not a personal attack or veiled insinuation about you, your life, or your activities. Avoid overgeneralizing and drawing conclusions based solely on what you think is being indirectly directed at you. The comments made by others are more often than not just what they are… comments, and they are not all about you.

Turn instead to an appreciation for the honest truth, live by it. Keep in mind that positive beliefs and thoughts are the ones that will carry you forward. While negative thoughts and beliefs lock you down and erode the miracle that you are.

Your beliefs and thoughts always thread through to your perceptions and then to your actions. It was Gautama Buddha who said,

With our thoughts
we make the world.

I would add to The Buddha's observation,

With your thoughts
you make your world.

Succumbing to negative thoughts telegraphs a lack of faith in the power of God, the Universe, the Source. Give pessimistic, fear-filled, unfounded, anxious thoughts no space inside your head. Monitor what you share with others, and avoid hosting debilitating habits. They are thieves. They steal from you. They can literally take your life.

Believe in yourself. Become all you can be. Monitor your thoughts and keep them on the high road as you await the arrival of a "want" on the Post-it note on the side of the refrigerator. Your next miracle or dream is on its way. Focus on that intention and in the meantime, enjoy yourself, love your life and your friends and family. Allow everyone to enjoy being around you.

8. Establish a belief system.

Establishing a belief system is in part like what I shared earlier about my art classroom rules. The last rule stated that each student's competition rested solely with him or her. Quickly they came to realize it was the most important and the most challenging of the three. Although they often struggled, they left at the end of each semester trusting their abilities and knowing why. Where their artistic talents and personal motivations were concerned, they had reached deep within themselves and ultimately developed healthy senses of self-esteem. They were proud of their achievements. They truly believed in themselves. With the establishment of a strong belief system comes a strong, healthy self-esteem.

You elected to come to Earth to experience specific circumstances and to grow spiritually. That is why you are here. You have the opportunity to take yourself to higher planes of understanding by following your Pathways with purpose and resolve. No matter what you think, you are here to teach yourself lessons. But, on this planet your biggest competition is always going to be you.

So, developing a personal belief system is worth your serious consideration. However, this could be the most complicated of the eight ideas for you to consider. This requires serious soul searching to develop.

Quite simply your belief system is:

- » what you truly believe
- » your personal values
- » your philosophy of life
- » the civilized creed by which you live
- » your views of how you fit into your environment

Belief systems can be secular or/and non-secular. They are not religious creeds. They are "you" creeds. They can certainly reflect your faith, but they go further than that.

Your belief system should be individualized and allow for fluidity. The 21st Century, British, philosopher, Stephen Law related belief systems to boats rather than to houses. Law feels they should have enough parts to always stay afloat, but enough flexibility to move as needs and experiences bring growth and/or changes. That is good advice.

Before you start to consider your personal belief system do not be misled into thinking your belief system is a religious sect. As in, if you are a member of a faith-based group that connection is your belief system. It is not. A group put that system together as a way to unify the whole. You are not a group.

According to authorities on the study of universal religions, there are currently nine, basic, organized, belief systems in the world. Soon there will be ten. Yours! It probably will not be "universal" but it will be organized for, and all about, just you.

Next, perhaps you think because you regularly attend a house of prayer or worship that it is your belief system. That building has a distinct purpose. It offers an opportunity for you to share in the celebration of your faith with others of common beliefs. However, that structure is not your personal belief system. Take a good look at it. It could be located on a lovely site, but it is a collection of stones and mortar and shingles and wood and glass and… . So, do not relax. You still need to develop your belief system, which is much more than the church, synagogue, temple, tent, or mosque you attend. It is more than the park bench you visit every Sunday morning to commune with nature.

Your belief system is what you believe. The way you think is best for you to live, to nurture your body, and enrich your soul. And keep in mind your belief system has to be YOU based. It has to be about what you put your faith and trust into every day.

Also, establishing a belief system is not about ways to bring others into your line of thinking. It should not be your ideas about the best way for the rest of the world to live. Your belief system is always all about you, even though it definitely reflects itself in how you treat others. Like it or not, you belief system is who you *really* are. The philosopher and writer, Ralph Waldo Emerson wrote,

The only person
you are destined to become
is the person
you decide to be.

If you are uncertain as to how to prepare a personal belief system, begin by asking yourself a basic but thought provoking question. Who are you? Ask yourself honestly and then actively seek the answers. Write them down. However, as you write, monitor your list for those entries that slip in and reflect how you think others see you. This list is for you and all about you. Recall the quotes regarding not succumbing to what others think about you that were written by R. Buckminster Fuller and Steve Jobs. On your list, no one's opinion counts but yours. Your life, your belief system, your relationship with your Source is yours. You are independent, accountable only to God, who has already accounted for you. He knew you before you were born. *The Old Testament's* book of Psalms 139:15-16 speaks of that,

My frame was not hidden from you,
when I was being made in secret,
intricately woven in the depths of the earth.
Your eyes beheld my unformed substance.
In your book were written
all the days that were formed for me,
when none of them as yet existed.

How beautifully and sensitively written that scripture reads when it says, *"In your book were written all the days that were formed for me, when none of them as yet existed."* Also, in *The Old Testament* the Prophet Isaiah wrote in Isaiah 43:1 of God's message to mankind,

I have called you by name
and you are mine.

Thomas Sweet, referred to that very scripture and the teachings of the early theologian John Calvin (1509-1564), a principal influence on Reformed Faith, when he said,

Knowing God and knowing ourselves
go hand in hand.
One cannot happen in any depth
without the other.

You are an integral part of the Universe, a part of God. To know yourself is to know your Creator. You are *in* this world, but not *of* this world. You are made from ages-old particles of the Universe. You are only visiting the planet Earth for a brief time. You intentionally arrived with a mission in mind. Your belief system is critical to successfully meeting your preordained objectives.

Like the third rule for my art students, this is one of the more significant actions to address in your life. In order for you to intentionally draw your "wants" to you, realize your dreams, and enjoy your desires on Spaceship Earth, it is critical that *you* know who you are. You are directly responsible for you. During your tenure you should make no excuses. You are a miracle on a mission.

The richness of life on this whirling planet is yours for the taking. Your predestined journey has the potential to bring you amazing adventures and wonderful opportunities. You can enjoy a glorious empowering relationship with this world and with your Creator.

Be the light others want to stand next to.

With God's blessing, follow your Pathways. Live your amazing life as the miracle that you are.

16

Concluding Thoughts

Determine to be, intend to be, and then become all you believe the miracle of you can be.

FASCINATING PEOPLE WERE SPRINKLED THROUGH the pages of *The Miracle of You*. They were selected so you could learn more about them *and* learn more about yourself. Some were intermittently flawed, like plunge-right-into-the-middle-of-things President Theodore "TR" Roosevelt and the periodically disgusted Prophet Moses and the fiery tempered Coach Vince Lombardi. Incredible human beings that they were, they were less than perfect, just as we are sometimes less than perfect.

Some individuals were noble beyond noble, such as Sihhartha Gautama Buddha, the Dalai Lama, and Jesus the Christ. Some people lived for nearly a century like the artist Marc Chagall and the cellist Pablo Casals. Others, like the child prodigy and maestro Wolfgang Amadeus Mozart and the famous writer Thomas Wolfe, lived only a few decades. During their lifetimes every person contributed exceptional gifts to their times… to all times. For being astronauts composed of stardust and over 13 billion years old, they did quite well.

In this book I intentionally moved from the remarkable miracle status of you to the miracles that come to you. Then on to the prearranged lesson plan you and God have for you. That plan includes living in joy. You brought joy with you to this lifetime. True joy, like pure love, is embedded in your soul. Joy is a priceless connector to your total being, to your highest self, to your oneness with the Universe.

Finally I focused on believing. You are responsible for knowing yourself and what you believe. Whether you actively practice an established faith or not, how can you, as a living miracle, exist in this amazing world and not give some thought as to what you believe? Or, give consideration to who you believe that you are?

No hyper-ego selfishness exists in focusing on building the miracle of you, because within you are the powers to do and be and give great gifts of yourself to yourself and to the world. Your goal in this life is the attainment of your loftiest Earth time experiences. If you believe, then you will achieve your dreams and fulfill your purpose.

Know that this planet, in fact this Universe, waits to be richly blessed by you. Contributing is a serious part of why you are here. No day takes you where tomorrow might lead. Your Pathways await your footsteps. Let one overriding thought linger,

You are the miracle
about whom this book was written.

The Miracle of You

A priceless,
irreplaceable treasure.
You are here
by divine grace.
Equipped with
unique talents and intentions.
Care for yourself
with gentleness and
generosity.
Bathe your blessed soul
in the wonderment
that is you.
Rejoice!

No one can do what you can do.
No one can be as you are.
You are a gift to the world.
You ARE a miracle.

You are a miracle on a mission.

Notes

Notes

Notes

Notes

Notes

Series Books by Elaine L Wilson

The Art of God's Message Series

Opening Doors

The Knight, Death and the Devil

Christian Symbolism, the art of Albrecht Durer

Until God So Wills

Abraham and the Three Angels

The life of Abraham, the art of Marc Chagall

Let There Be Light

The Moses window

Stained glass by L. B. Saint, the life of Moses,
The National Cathedral, Washington, DC

Messengers of Miracles

The Pieta

The Virgin Mary, the sculpture of Michelangelo

Coming Home

The Return of the Prodigal Son

Images of Christ, the art of Rembrandt

Transcending Time

The Penitent Magdalene

Mary Magdalene, the art of Georges de LaTour

The Passion of the Soul

The Last Supper

The 12 Apostles, the art of Leonardo da Vinci

Look to the Shore

Christ at the Sea of Galilee

The miracles of Jesus, the art of Tintoretto

Leaving Legacies

The Conversion on the Road to Damascus

The Apostle Paul, the art of Michelangelo Caravaggio

Present at the Table

The Eucharist

The meaning of communion, the art of Salvador Dali

Another World

The Sistine Chapel ceiling

The images and panels on the ceiling,
the art of Michelangelo

A Second Chance

The Rising of Lazarus

The Seven Mighty Miracles of Jesus,
the art of Michelangelo Caravaggio

Iconically Speaking

The Trinity icon

Russian icons and cathedrals,
the art of Andrei Rublev

Shining Lights

The history of the cross, the art of El Greco,
the poetry of St. John of the Cross

Amidst the Stars

Noli Me Tangere

The appearance in the garden, the art of Titian

Other Books by Elaine L Wilson

In Praise
The Psalms in Word and Image
The words of King David,
free verse poetry,
photographs of the USA

Other Shores
Life's Changing Journey
Short stories about the next shores we move toward as life brings changes and awakenings to our lives.

Your Favorite Guest
An exceptional and beautifully illustrated cookbook of delicious, easy to prepare, uncomplicated recipes straight from (my Mom) Tressa's kitchen.

About the Author

An accomplished lecturer and the author of 18 other books, ***Elaine L Wilson*** holds BS and MS degrees from Indiana University of Pennsylvania and Pennsylvania State University, respectively. She attained advanced Administrative Supervisory Certification at Temple University.

She is the founder and past Executive Director of the Susquehanna Art Museum in Harrisburg PA.

Working with Russian counter-parts, Elaine co-founded the first two private schools in the USSR in Moscow, Russia. She sat on the Executive Committee for the Pennsylvania Art Education Association, has served on a number of local and statewide boards, and is Director of Adult Education and a ruling Elder with her church. She is a former art educator and K-12 Art Supervising Administrator.

As a watercolor artist, she has exhibited in both group and

one-person shows. Her art is in private collections in the USA and Europe.

Her current interests revolve around traveling, painting, writing, and lecturing.

She resides in south central Pennsylvania in the USA.

About the Artwork

My earliest artistic effort (of note) was drawn with a bright green crayon all over the back of my parents' just-purchased, long, white sofa. My punishment for surprising the family with such a brilliant masterpiece was to sit on a chair and stare at my efforts for half an hour. I was directed by my Mother to "Think about what you have done." I was 3-years old at the time. Perhaps it was then that I determined the course of one of my future, professional, career Pathways. It had to include the field of creative expression. As for the drawing-all-over-the-back-of-the-new-sofa discipline, I have never stopped drawing and painting. However, I continue to control my urges to drawn on the backs of any more furniture.

To help support my financial needs during college, I turned to my artistic talents. Those years included a myriad of opportunities to paint for profit. None of which lent much glamour to my life, but they did provide some income. I painted lettering on school buses, dump trucks, highway construction site billboards, race track signs, and store front windows.

During my tenure in public education, I used my artist talents as a form of therapy. Sitting down with a palette loaded with paint, a clean white surface, and a fist-full of brushes can be a delightful away to cool down from the issues of earlier in any day. And, that habit lead to future exhibits and one-person shows of my art. That was a true bonus. I still paint in watercolor, when I am not writing books. Both creative expressions are demanding and require focus. I can only handle one at a time.

The artworks in this book are watercolor paintings. The sizes of the originals vary from 14 x 24-inches to 3 x 6-inches. I selected the images to support my personal quips under each image. I introduced the statements to set the tone for each chapter.

Good friends should give you space to breathe and freely consider. I believe good books should give readers opportunities to pause and reflect in the process of reading and learning.

Elaine L Wilson